Derricks 1
Derrick 2
Derrick 3
デリック 4

DINOSAUR
CARTON CRAFT

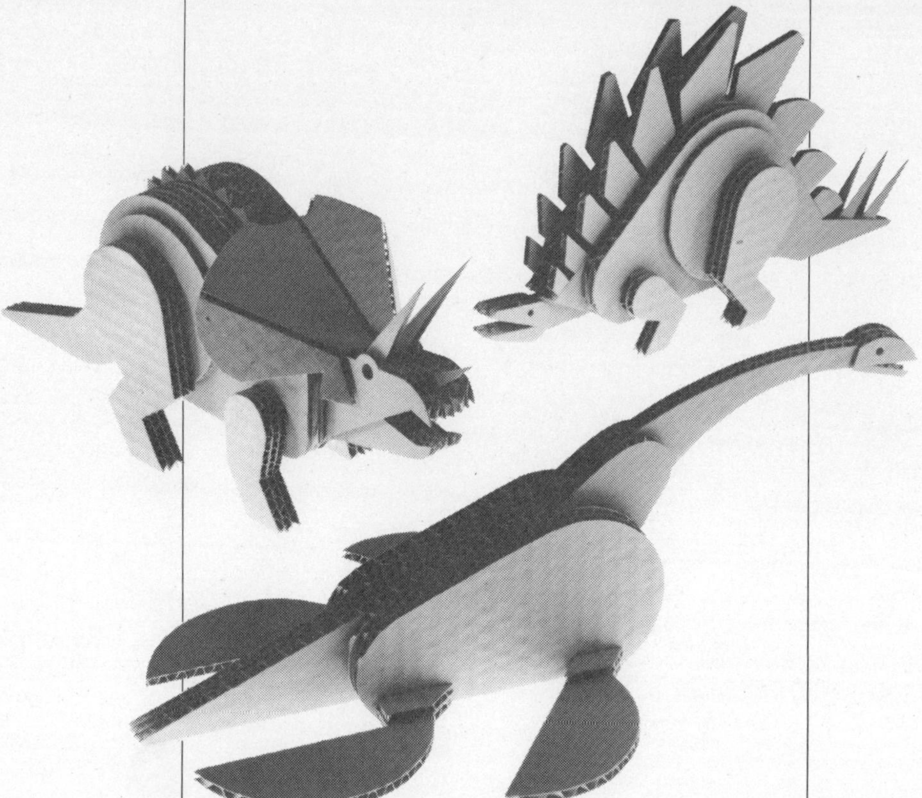

HIDEHARU NAITOH

Published by Seibundo Shinkosha Publishing Co., Ltd.
13-7, Yayoicho 1-chome, Nakano-ku, Tokyo, 164 Japan

Distributors:
UNITED STATES: *Kodansha America, Inc., through Farrar, Straus & Giroux, 19 Union Square West, New York, NY 10003.*
CANADA: *Fitzhenry & Whiteside Ltd., 91 Granton Drive, Richmond Hill, Ontario L4B 2N5.*
BRITISH ISLES AND EUROPEAN CONTINENT: *Premier Book Marketing Ltd., 1 Gower Street, London WC1E 6HA.*
AUSTRALIA AND NEW ZEALAND: *Bookwise International, 54 Crittenden Road, Findon, South Australia 5023.*
THE FAR EAST AND JAPAN: *Japan Publications Trading Co., Ltd., 1-2-1, Sarugaku-cho, Chiyoda-ku, Tokyo 101.*

First edition: September 1992

ISBN 0-87040-911-5

Printed in Japan

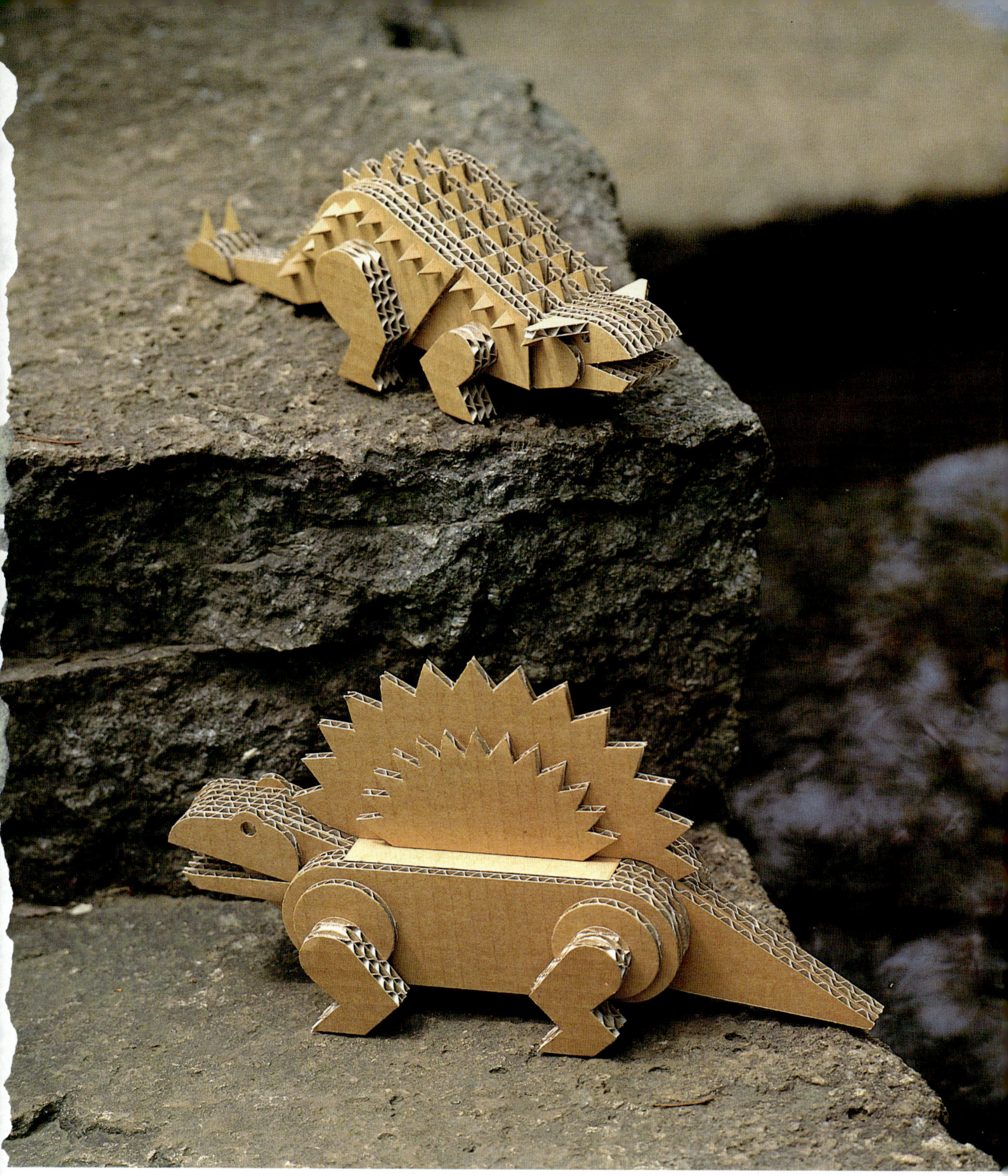

SCOLOSAURUS (TOP) **DIMETRODON** (BOTTOM)

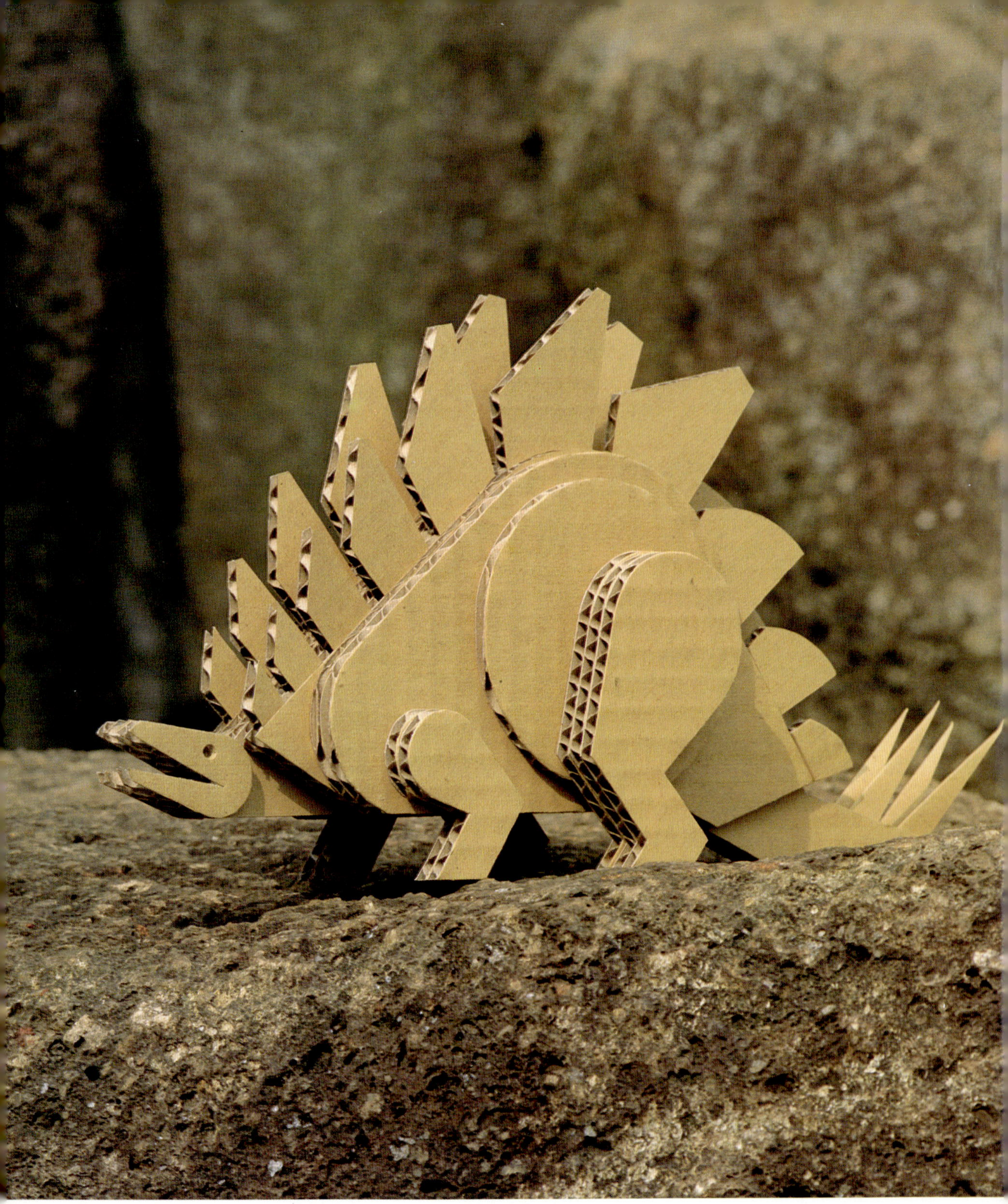

STEGOSAURUS (L)　　**PARASAUROLOPHUS** (R)

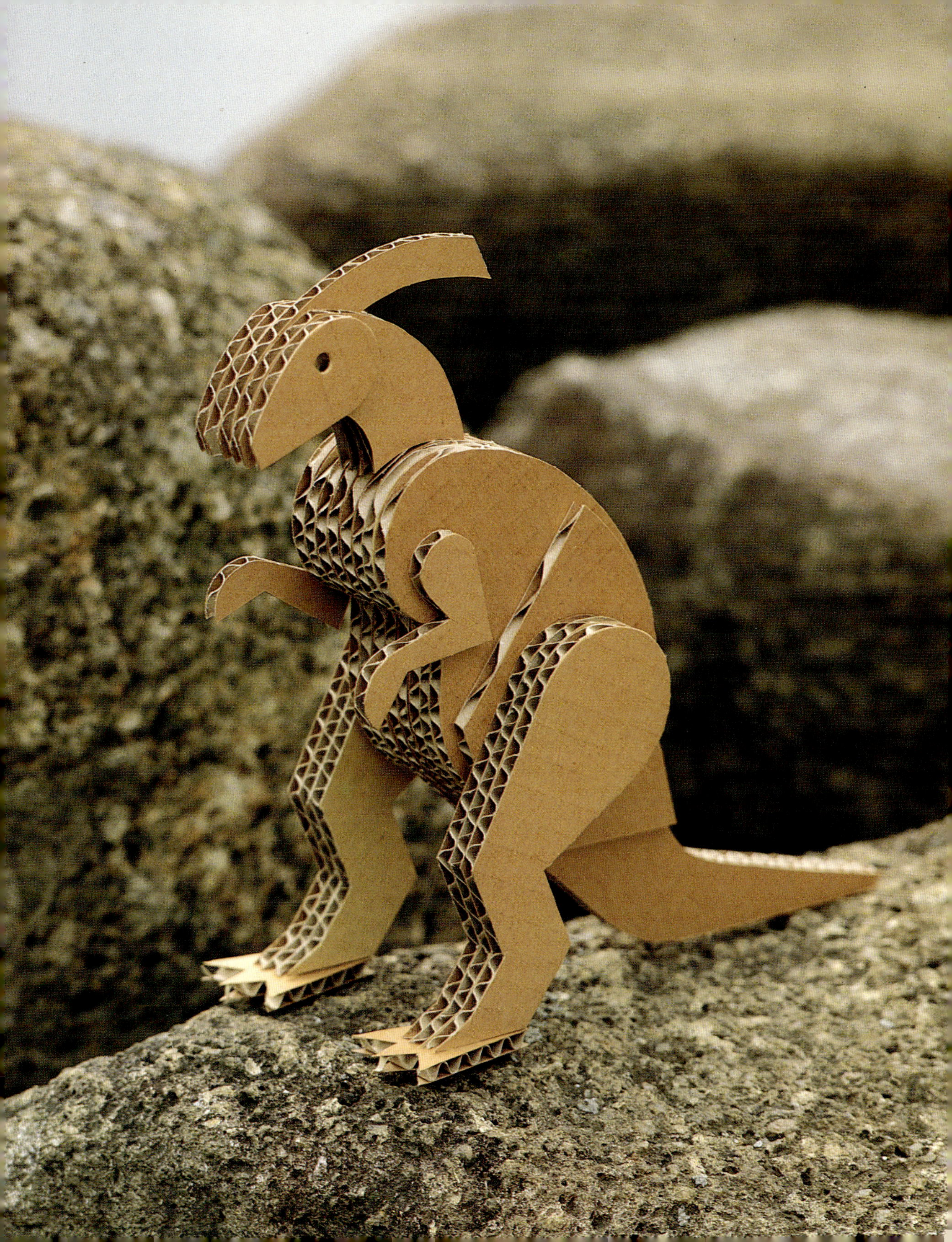

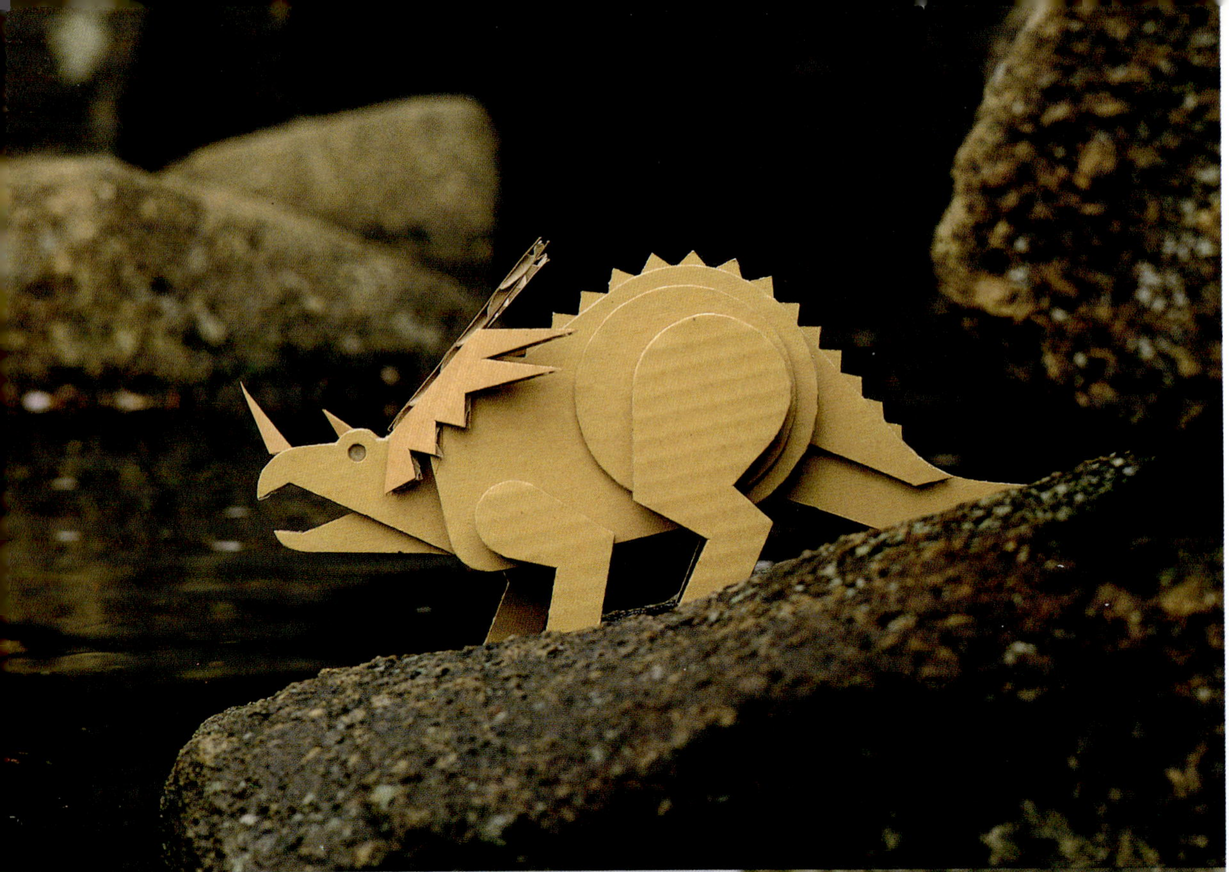

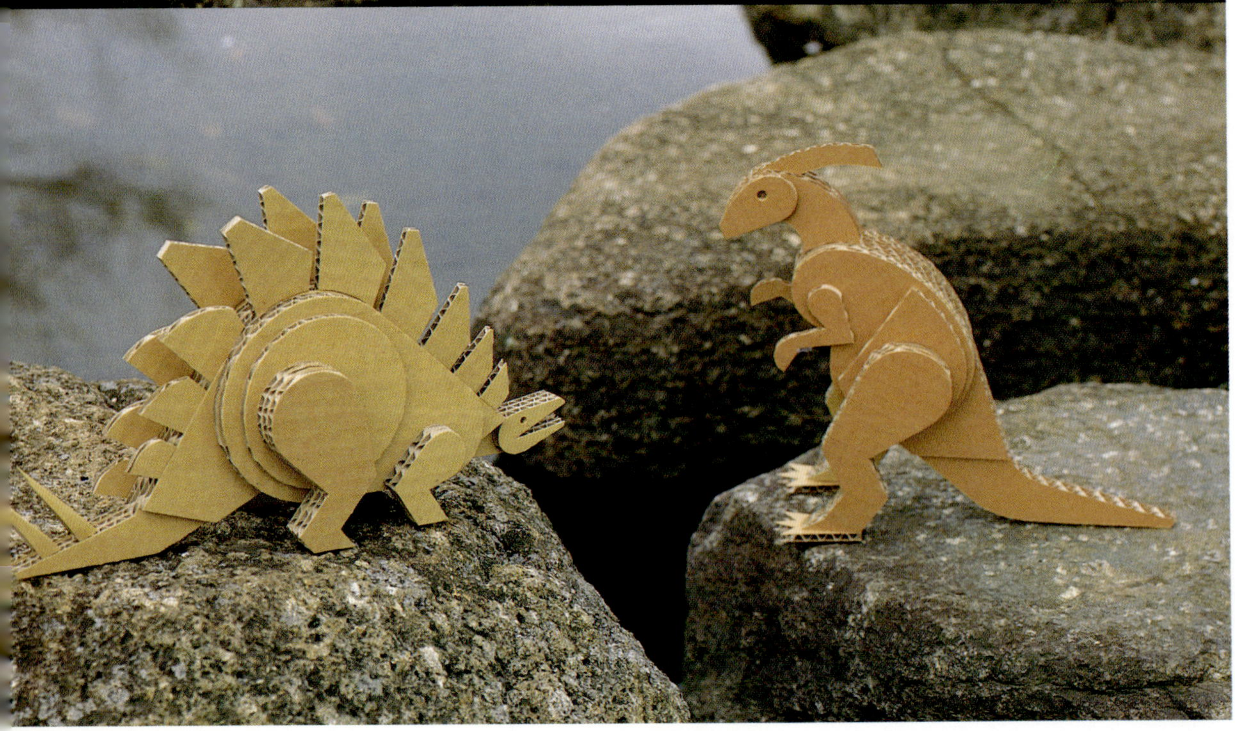

STYRACOSAURUS (TOP) **STEGOSAURUS** (BOTTOM·L) **PARASAUROLOPHUS** (BOTTOM·R)

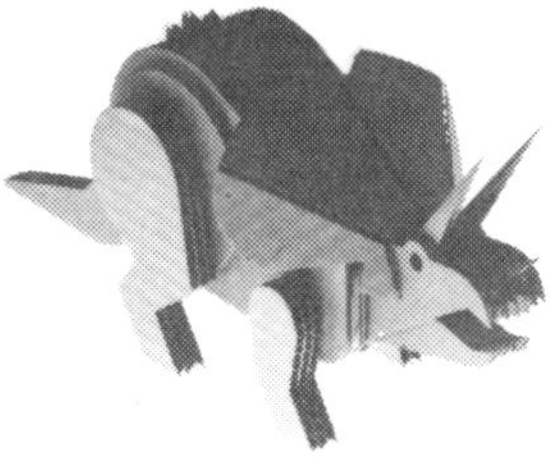

DINOSAUR
CARTON CRAFT

Contents

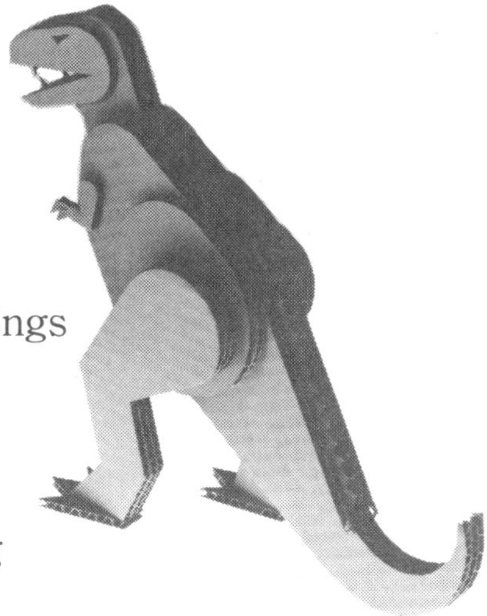

2 ········ About cardboard
4 ········ Tools and materials
5 ········ Using other materials
6 ········ How to copy the drawings
8 ········ Cutting technique
10 ········ Basics of assembly
11 ········ Varnishing and coloring
12 ········ Plesiosaurus
17 ········ Pteranodon
23 ········ Parasaurolophus
29 ········ Scolosaurus
35 ········ Triceratops
41 ········ Styracosaurus
44 ········ Stegosaurus
50 ········ Dimetrodon (Pencil Holder)
56 ········ Tyrannosaurus

ABOUT CARDBOARD

These days, empty cardboard boxes abound in most people's homes, since electronic and household goods usually come packed in them. Sometimes they get used again as toy boxes or for storing old clothes, but that is usually the extent of it. As a result, extra boxes often end up being thrown away. This is especially true at supermarkets and shopping centers where unwanted boxes tend to pile up.

Until recently, cardboard was considered to be old, dirty or low-grade paper, but with growing ecological consciousness, people are rediscovering its value and finding ways to get maximum use out of it.

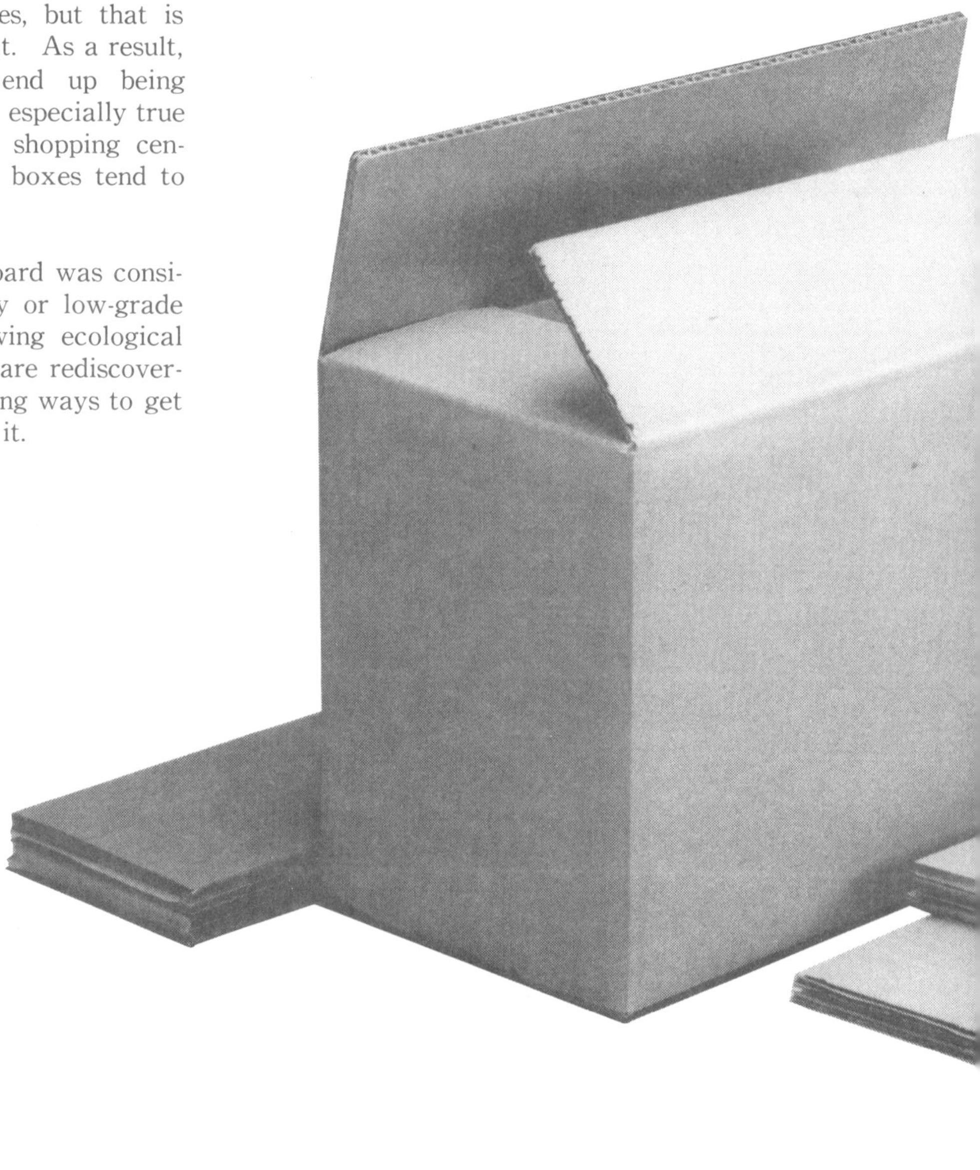

Our way of thinking has been changing, towards more natural tastes. We are more aware of the environment, and we can recognize now what a great resource cardboard really is. Empty cardboard boxes are not just garbage, but recyclable materials for making things like carton craft.

This book is not only for children but for people of all ages who enjoy making crafts. While grade school children will find it easier to cut out the patterns made with straight lines, the more complicated patterns with lots of curved lines will appeal to older students and adults. With a little time and effort, anyone can make quality carton craft.

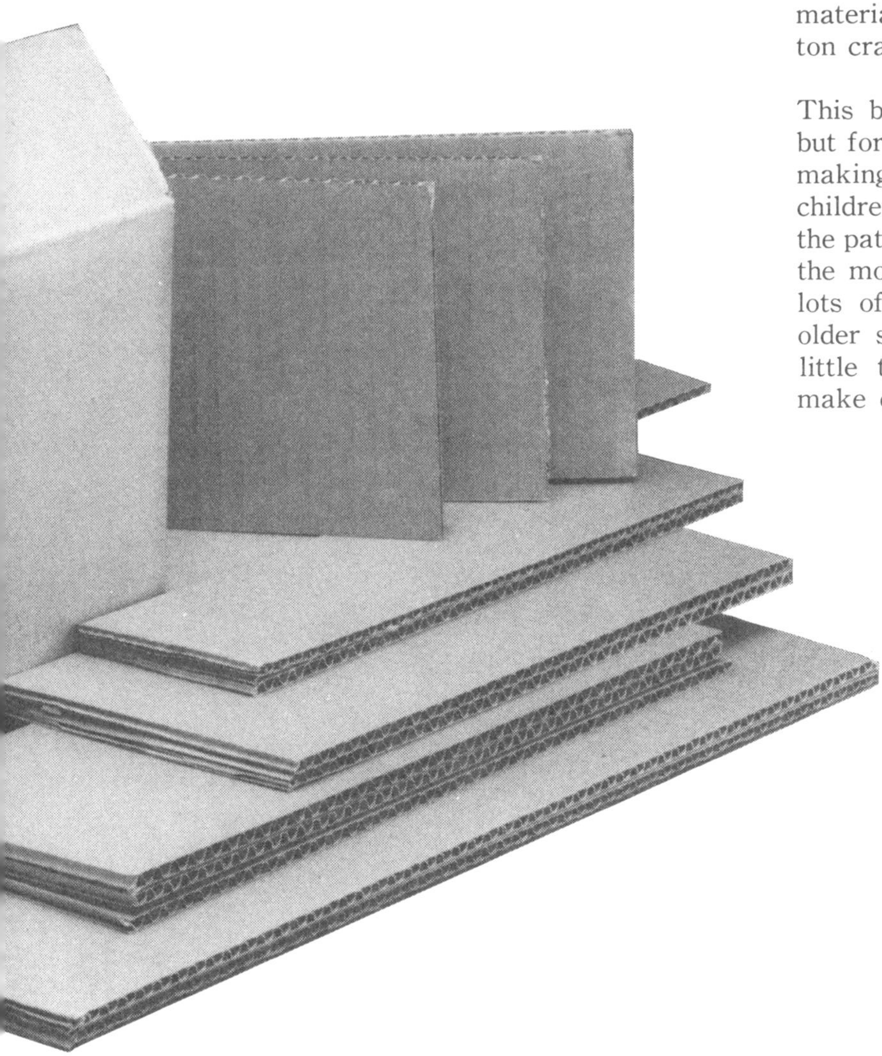

TOOLS AND MATERIALS

In terms of tools and materials, you will not need anything out of the ordinary. You will use things that you probably already use at your school or home. Naturally it is best if you use tools that you are accustomed to. Handle your craft work carefully and efficiently and you will not be disappointed. You might even surprise yourself! A word about glue: although any kind of glue will do. I use wood glue. Use ordinary, flat, currogated cardboard. Your blade will cut through $\frac{1}{8}$" to $\frac{1}{4}$" (3mm-5mm) thick cardboard, but will not cut through multiple layers.

Tools and Materials:

- Pencil (F, HB, B-6B)
- Cutter (with extra blades)
- Small scissors
- Compass
- Rulers (straight, triangular)
- Tweezers
- Eyeletteer (for making holes)
- Glue (wood glue is best)
- Cellophane tape
- Cutting board or rubber mat
- Tracing paper (graphlined)
- Carbon paper
- Cardboard, flat, currogated, ($\frac{1}{4}$"/5mm thick)
- Wooden sticks ($\frac{1}{4}$"/5mm diam.)
- Toothpicks (round)

(Wood not needed for dinosaurs)

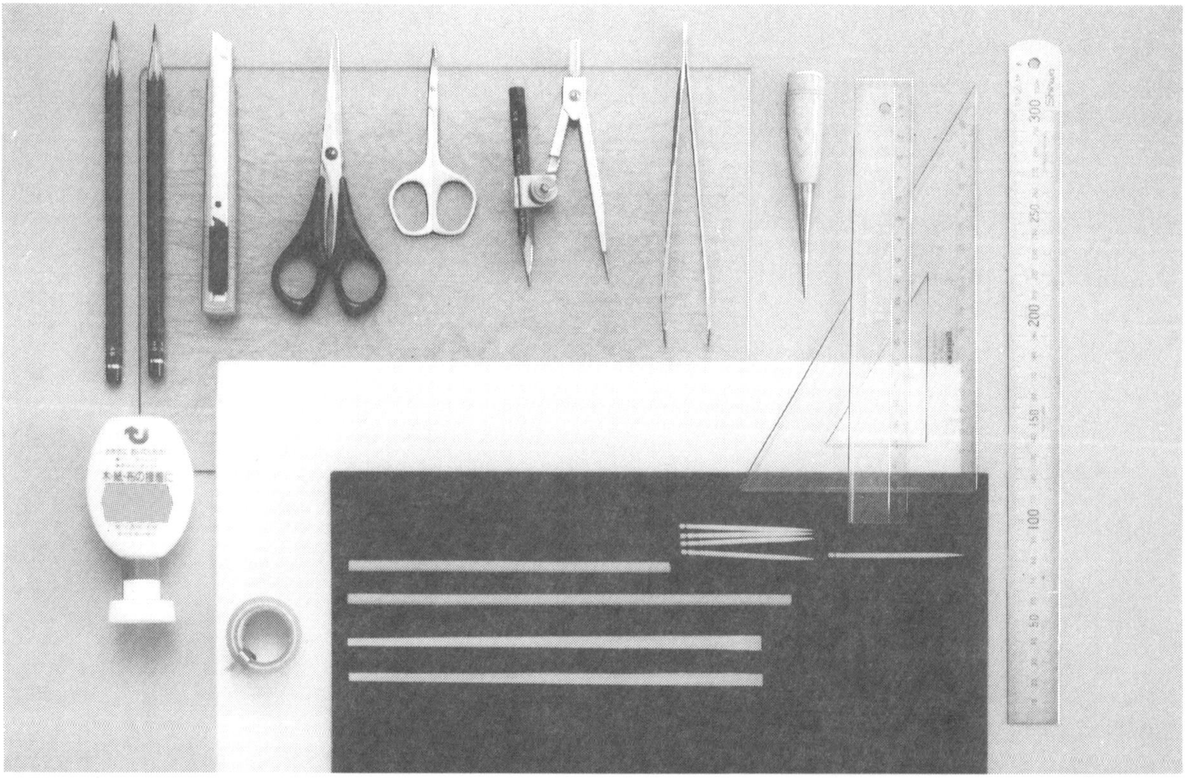

USING OTHER MATERIALS

When making carton craft with this book, you can substitute other materials for cardboard. As long as the building materials, such as balsa wood, cork or styrofoam (see photo) are about $\frac{1}{4}$" (5mm) thick, your blade should cut through them quite easily. There are all kinds of carton craft that you can make, and by choosing different materials and variations, you can design one-of-a-kind creations.

Some ideas of things to try:

- change straight lines into curved lines or vice versa
- make the shape longer or shorter
- decrease or increase the number of layers
- add or omit wheels
- roll wheels, moving parts
- make it bigger or smaller
- make it with just one kind of side part
- try making the torso hollow to store small objects
- use 2 types of materials
- create your own designs

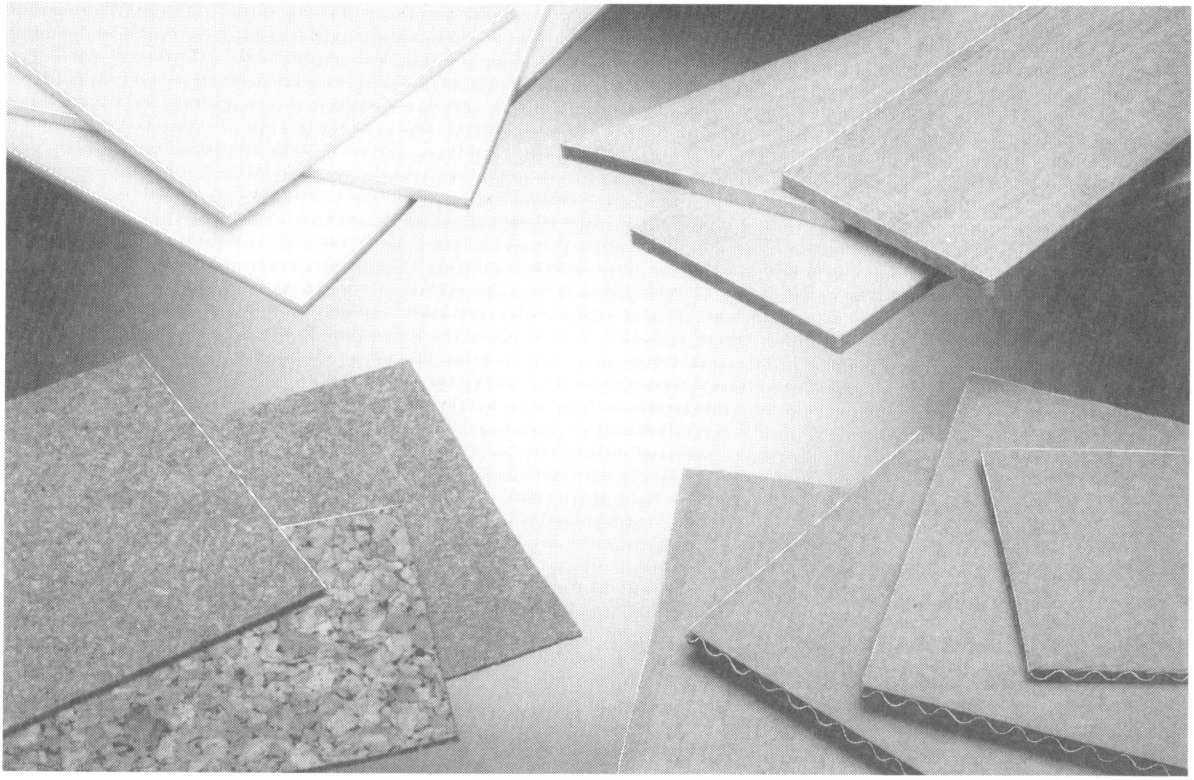

HOW TO COPY THE DRAWINGS

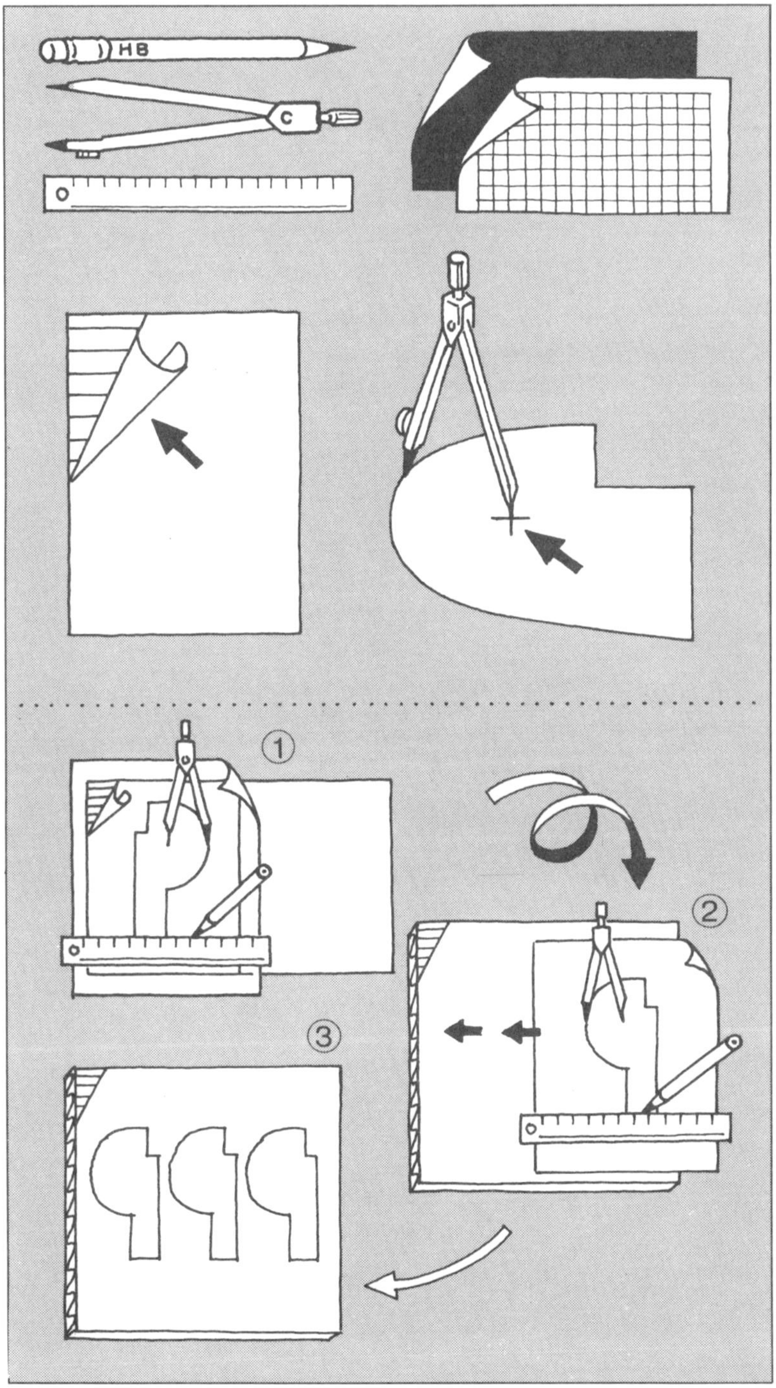

MATERIALS AND TOOLS
HB pencil, compass, ruler, carbon paper, tracing paper (preferably with graph lines).

The lines drawn in the upper corner of each actual-size drawing show the direction of the cardboard currogation. When tracing the drawings onto the cardboard, be sure that the direction of the cardboard matches that in the drawing.

The cross marks which appear alone or in the center of circular sections are very useful when copying with a compass.

HOW TO COPY USING PENCIL
① Lay the tracing paper (preferably with graphlines) on top of the actual-size drawing, and with the help of a compass and ruler, trace the image with an HB pencil.
② Turn the tracing paper over onto the cardboard, making sure that the grain of the cardboard is the same direction as in the drawing. Transfer the image onto the cardboard by tracing along the pencil line.
③ Trace the needed number of parts onto the cardboard.

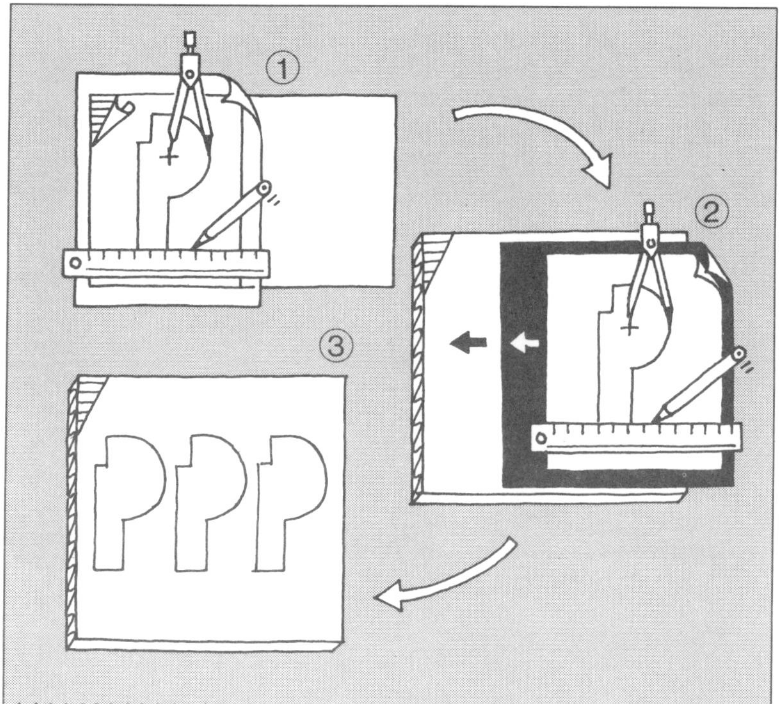

HOW TO COPY USING CARBON PAPER

① Lay the graph-lined tracing paper on top of the actual-size drawing and with the help of a compass and ruler, trace the image with an HB pencil.

② Place carbon paper between the tracing paper and the cardboard. Trace over the image to transfer it.

③ Trace the needed number of pieces onto the cardboard.

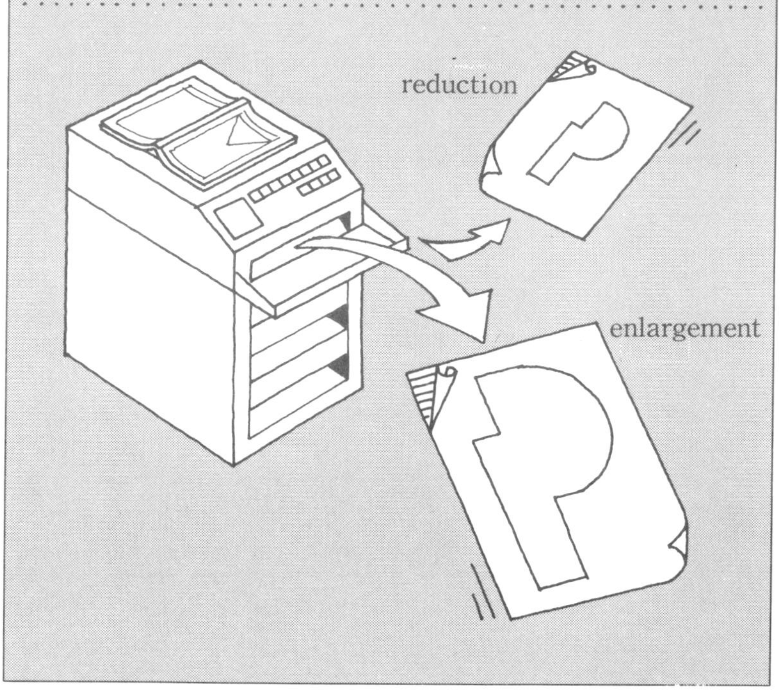

REDUCING AND ENLARGING

Using a photocopier, you can enlarge or reduce the size of the diagrams, and then trace them the same way. It's fun to make big dinosuars, too!

CUTTING TECHNIQUE

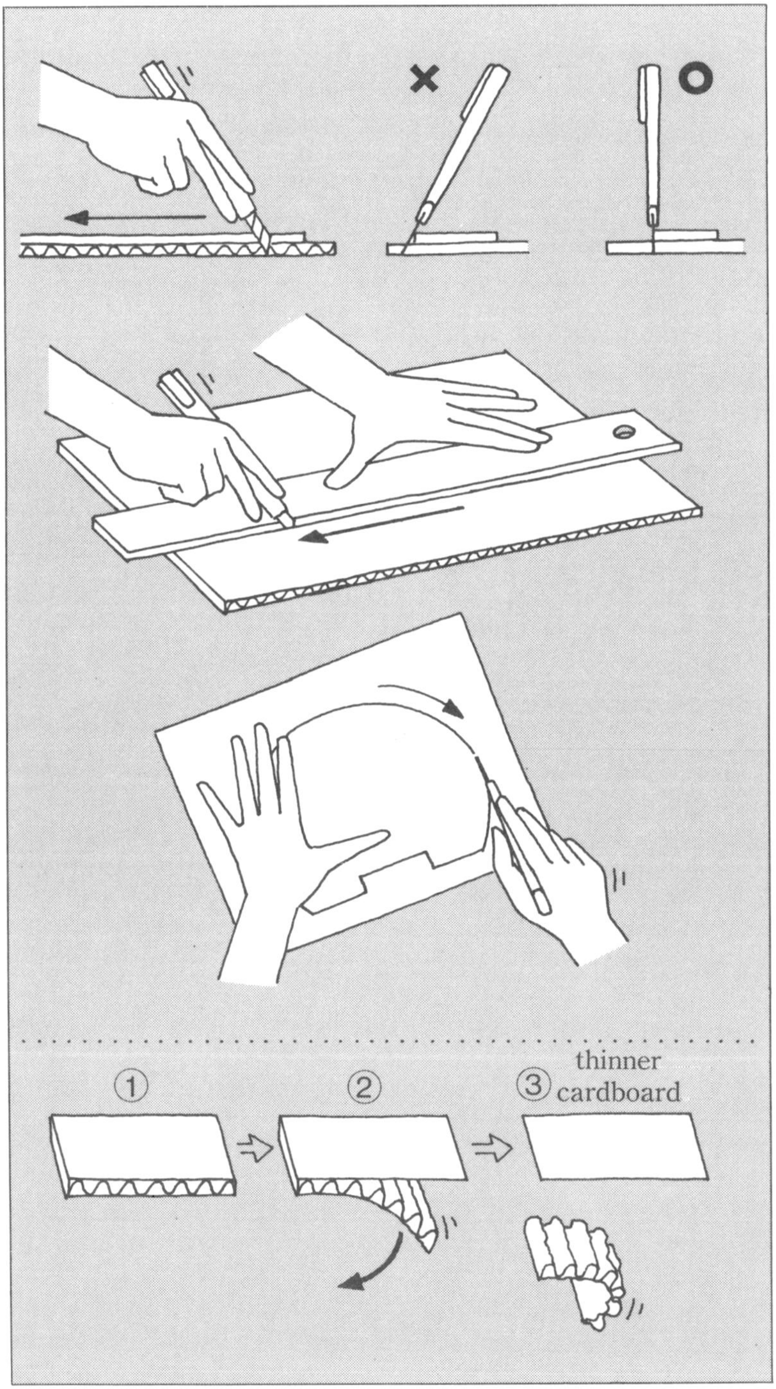

HOW TO HOLD THE CUTTER
Hold the cutter as shown in the diagram, and draw it along the cardboard 3 to 5 times to cut right through.

*If the blade on your cutter becomes even a little dull, break it off and use a new blade.

*Be sure to place a cutting board or rubber mat underneath what you are cutting.

CUTTING STRAIGHT LINES
As in the diagram, use a ruler, and slowly, carefully cut along the line. (Metal rulers are very good for this.)

CUTTING LARGE CURVES
Holding the cutter in a free-hand fashion, pass over the line 3 to 5 times to cut it through.

REMOVING THE OUTER PAPER FROM THE CARDBOARD (TO USE ON ITS OWN)
① Cut the small piece of cur-rogated cardboard needed.
② Peel off the outer layer of paper perpendicularly to the currogation's grain.
③ Or, if possible, just cut through the thick paper on one side of the cardboard.

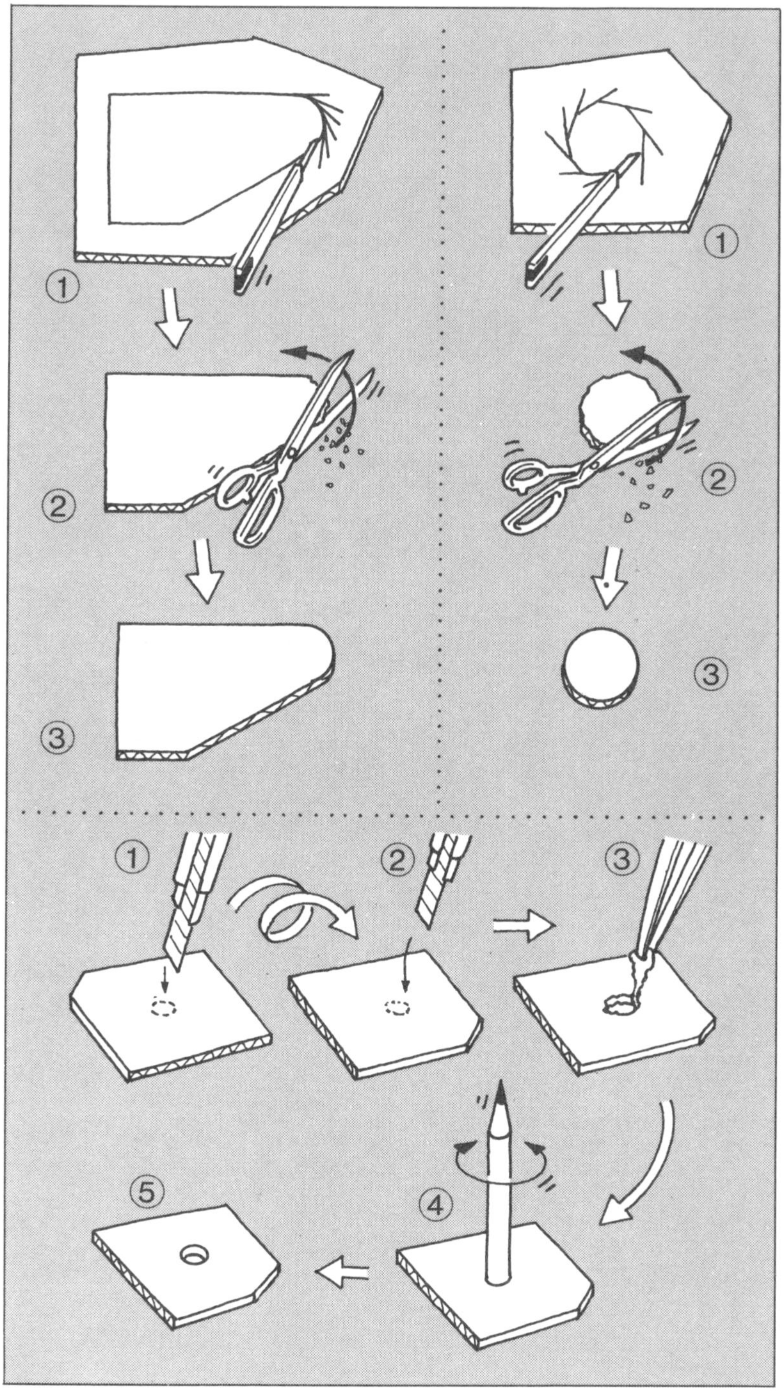

CUTTING SMALL CURVES

① As shown in the diagram, first make a series of small straight cuts all the way around.

② Then, using scissors, round off the edges.

③ Finished

MAKING SMALL HOLES

① Using the tip of the cutter to pierce the cardboard, cut along the edge of the hole.

② Turn the cardboard over and cut the same way on the other side.

③ Using a pair of tweezers, carefully pull out the middle part.

④ As shown in the diagram, put a pencil in the hole and twist it around.

⑤ Finished

BASICS OF ASSEMBLY

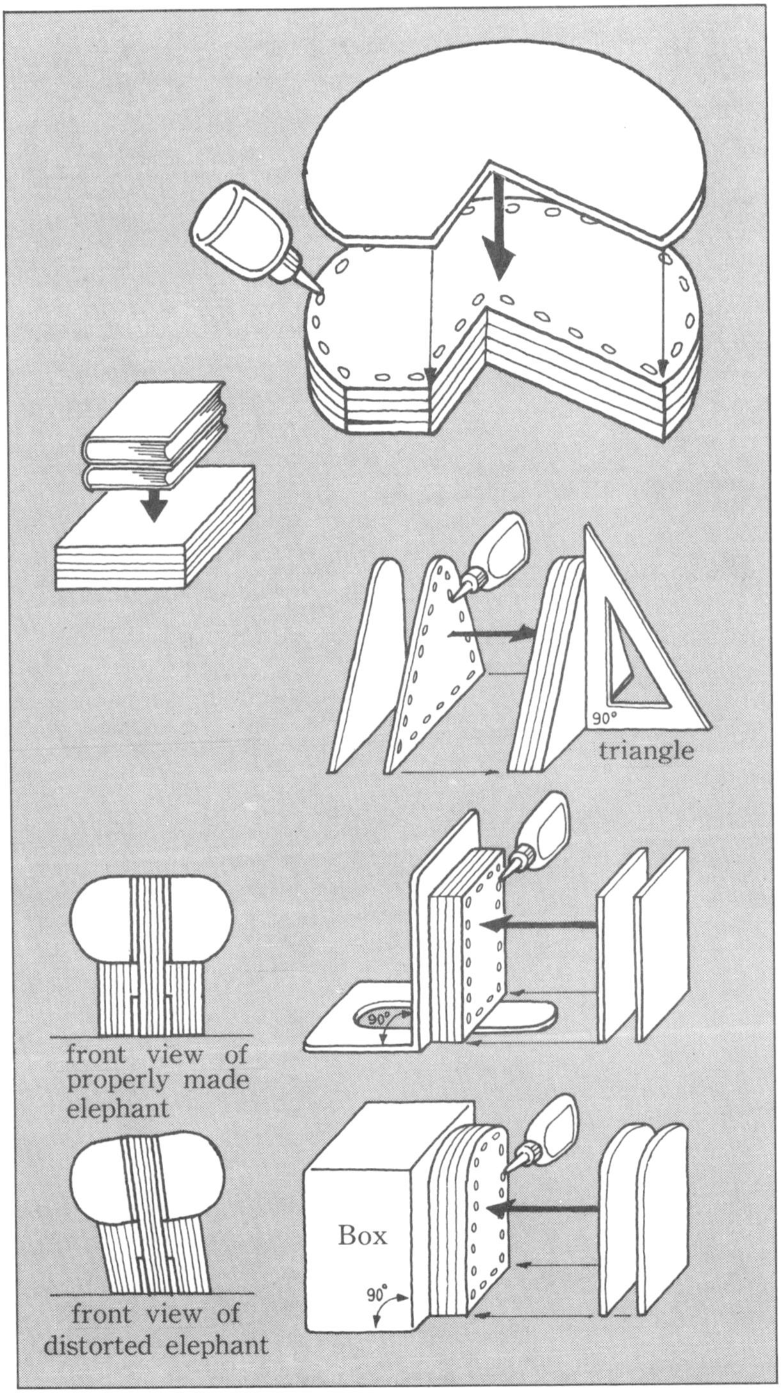

When gluing pieces together, dab the glue around the edge at intervals of $\frac{1}{4}''$ to $\frac{1}{2}''$ (5mm to 10mm) as the diagram shows.

Caution: Be sure not to overglue. If you use too much glue, it will bulge out and take too long to dry.

To correct warping, and to help them adhere, carefully pile 2 or 3 thick books on top of the glued parts and let sit for about 5 minutes.

When gluing parts in a vertical position, use a triangle, a book-stand or a box to keep everything completely straight.
This is the most important point for making good carton craft. Calmly, slowly and carefully glue the pieces together.

VARNISHING AND COLORING

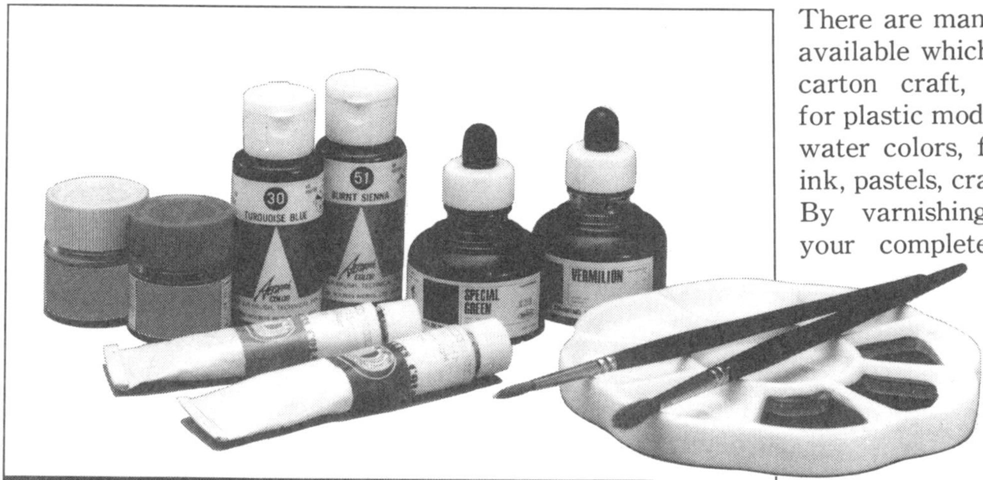

There are many types of paints available which can be used for carton craft, including paints for plastic models, poster paints, water colors, felt pens, colored ink, pastels, crayons and so on. By varnishing or lacquering your completed carton craft, you add color and texture to the cardboard, and can even make it look like wood. Also, a glossy finish will add to its durability. There are all kinds of finishing products on the market, from transparent and light brown to dark brown, so feel free to experiment.

Caution: When diluting with paint thinner, do so only under well-ventilated conditions and always be fire conscious.

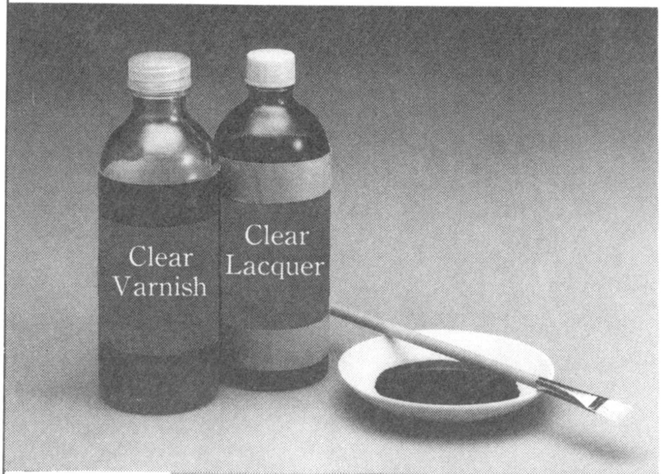

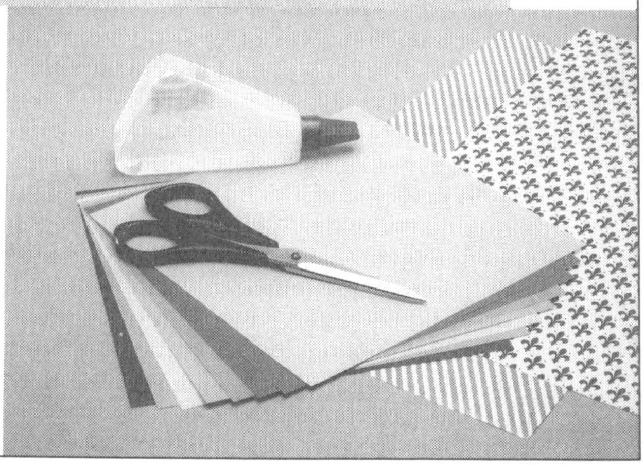

It is also interesting to glue colored paper or colorful wrapping paper onto your carton craft.

PLESIOSAURUS

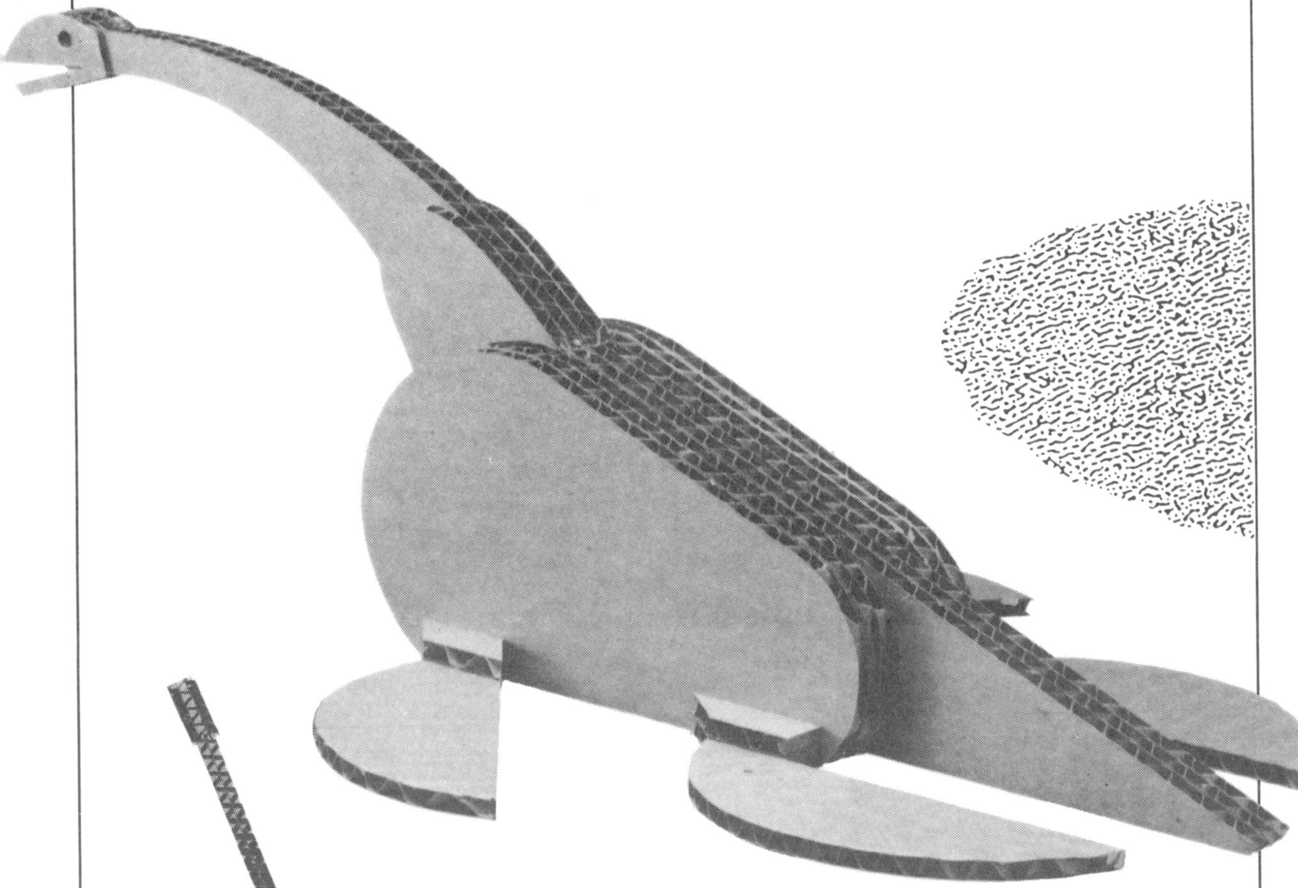

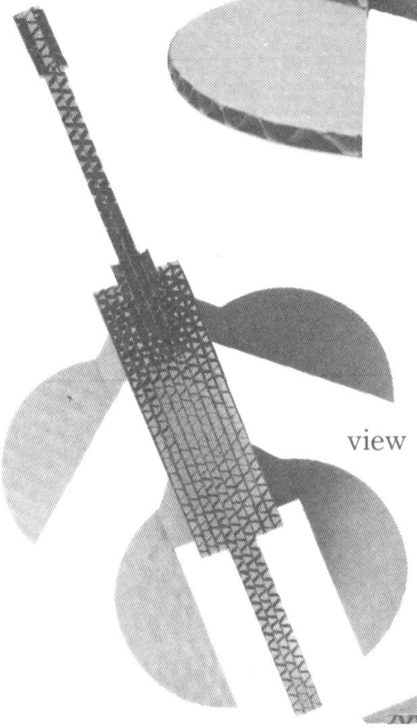

view from above

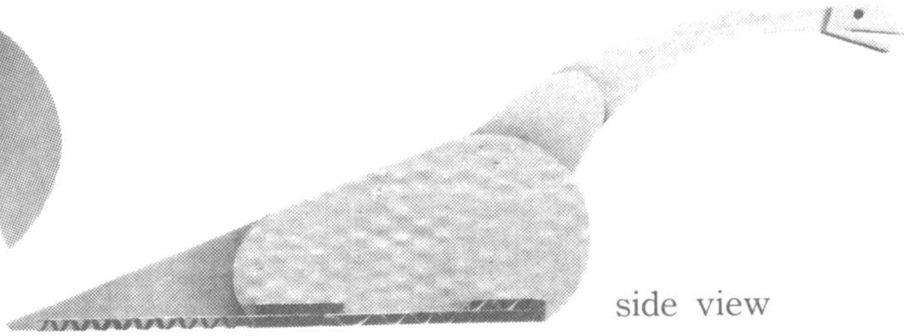

side view

PLESIOSAURUS = ACTUAL-SIZE DRAWING〔 I 〕

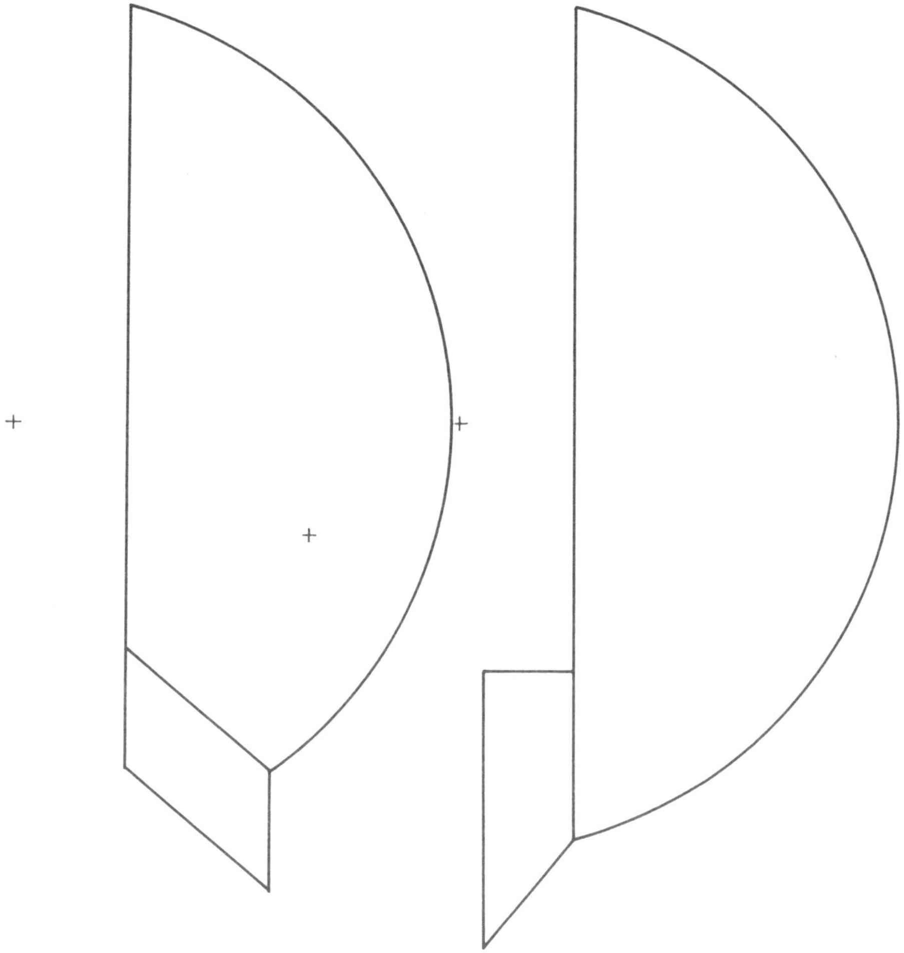

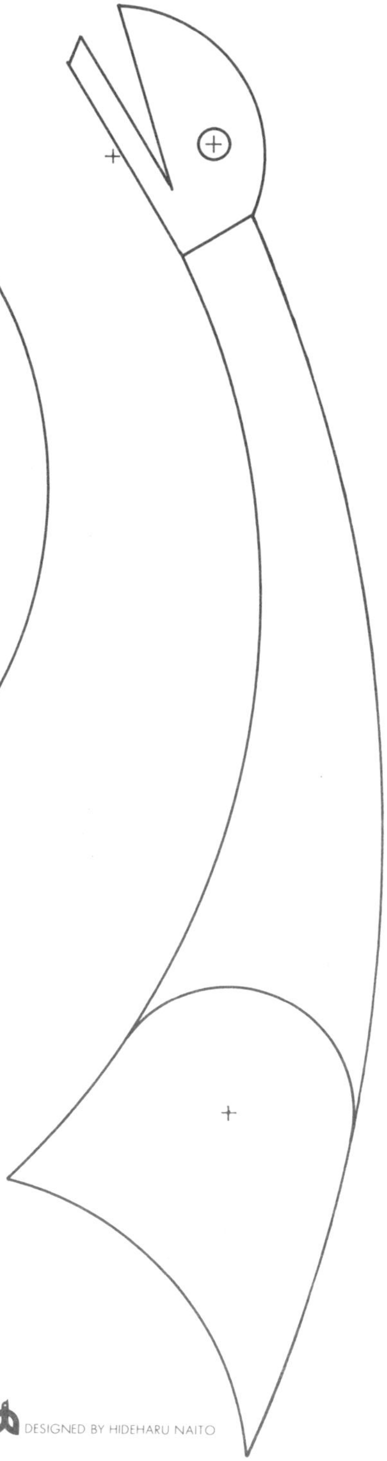

★Idea sketch★

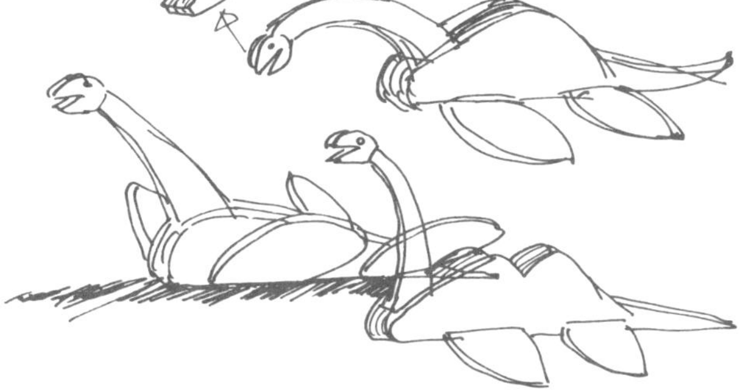

DESIGNED BY HIDEHARU NAITO

PLESIOSAURUS = ACTUAL-SIZE DRAWING〔II〕

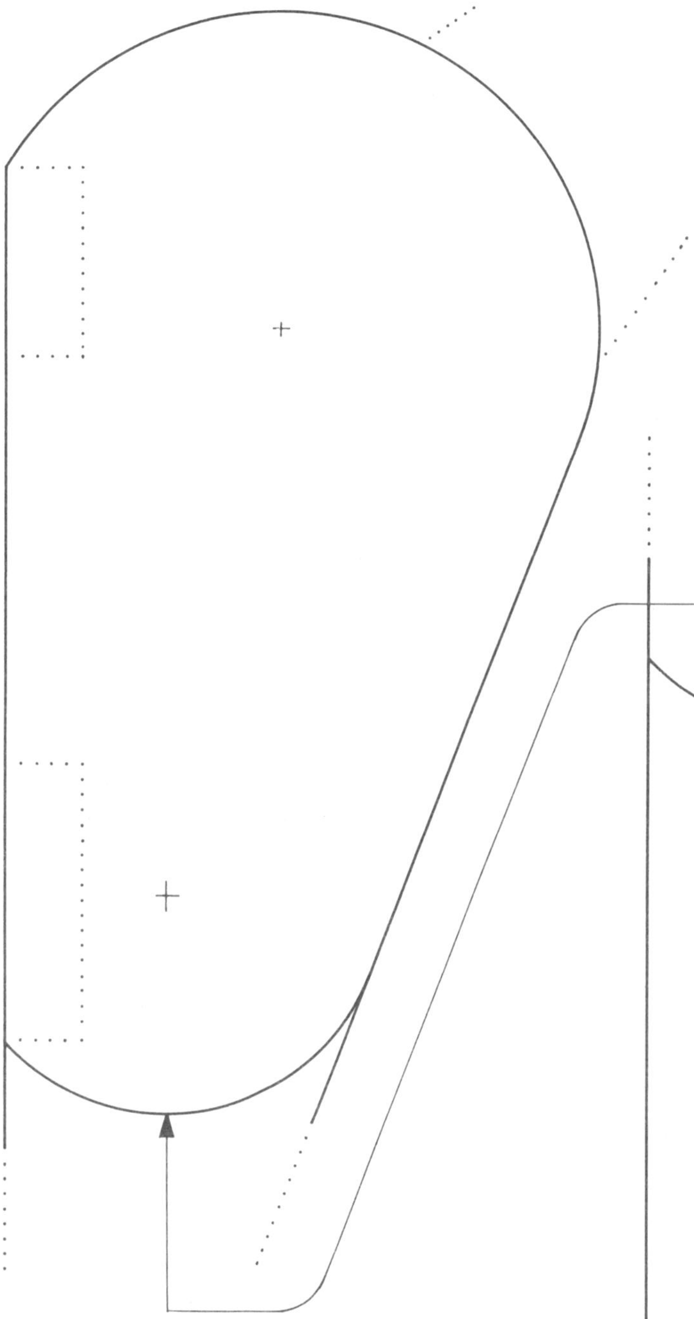

When tracing, place the drawing on the right under this curved line to create one drawing.

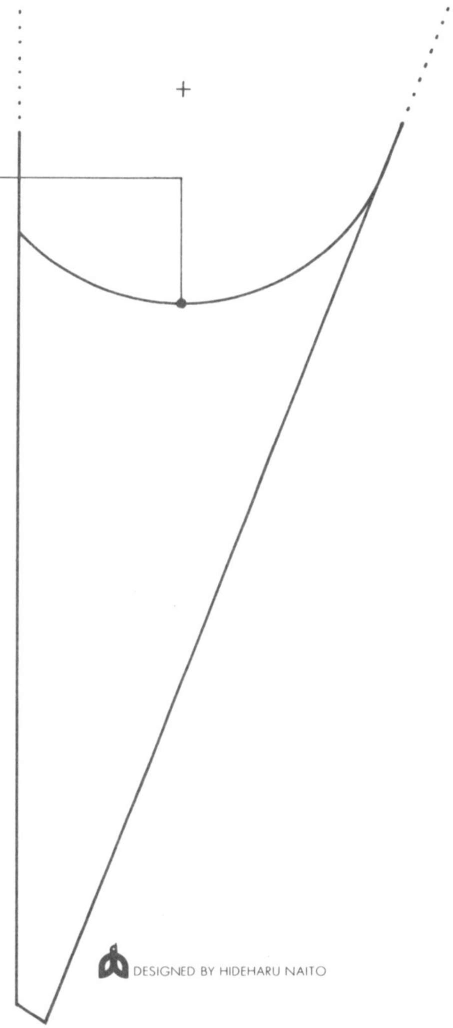

DESIGNED BY HIDEHARU NAITO

★ Double-check the number of parts

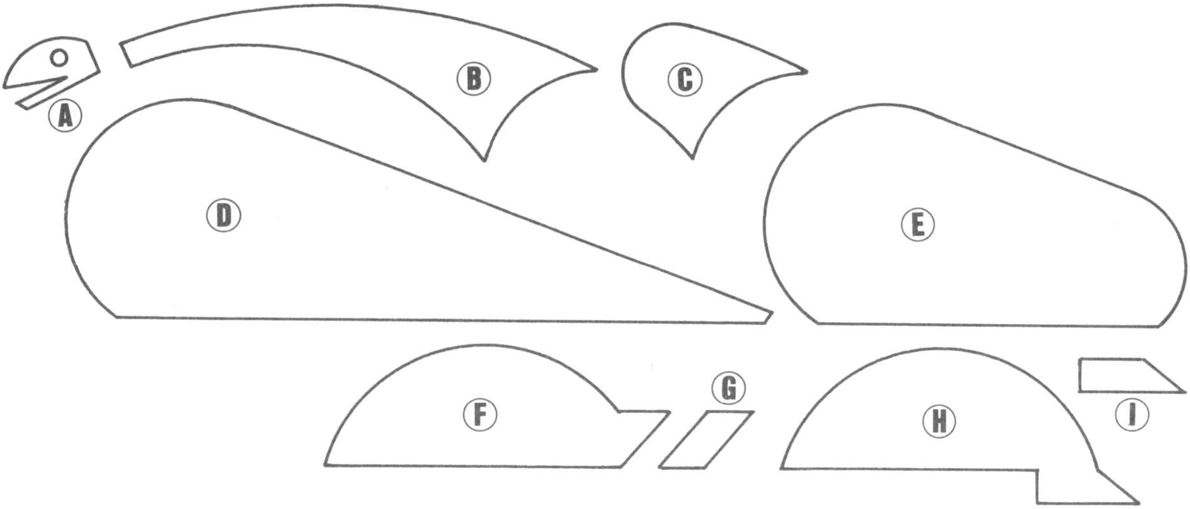

Ⓐ×3 (but cut eyes in only 2) Ⓑ×2 Ⓒ×2
Ⓓ×3 Ⓔ×6 Ⓕ×2 Ⓖ×2 Ⓗ×2 Ⓘ×2

1

To build the torso, glue the 3 Ⓓ pieces together. Then glue the Ⓔ parts together in 2 piles of 3 each. Next, as in the diagram, glue the Ⓔ sections to either side of the Ⓓ section.

Dab the glue at intervals of $\frac{1}{4}$" to $\frac{1}{2}$" (5mm to 10mm), and use a triangle to be sure that the pieces are vertical.

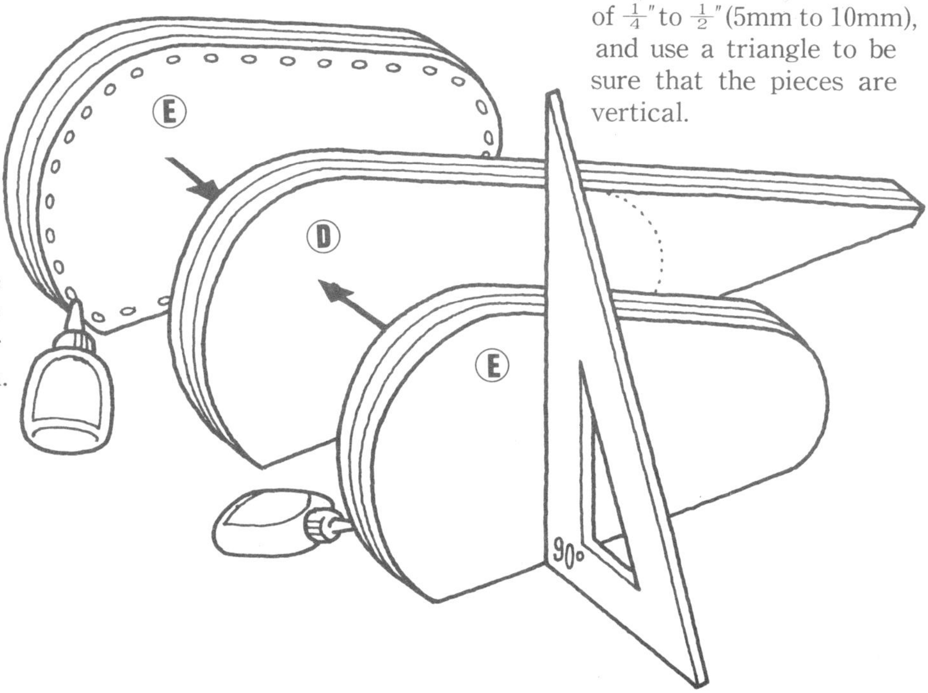

2

Glue the 3 Ⓐ parts of the head together. Glue the 2 Ⓑ parts of the neck together, and then glue on the left and right sides of the base of the neck Ⓒ. Then, as shown in the diagram, connect the head to the neck.

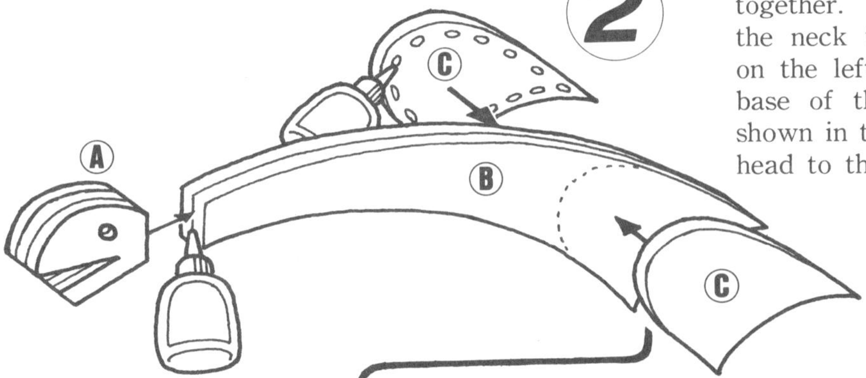

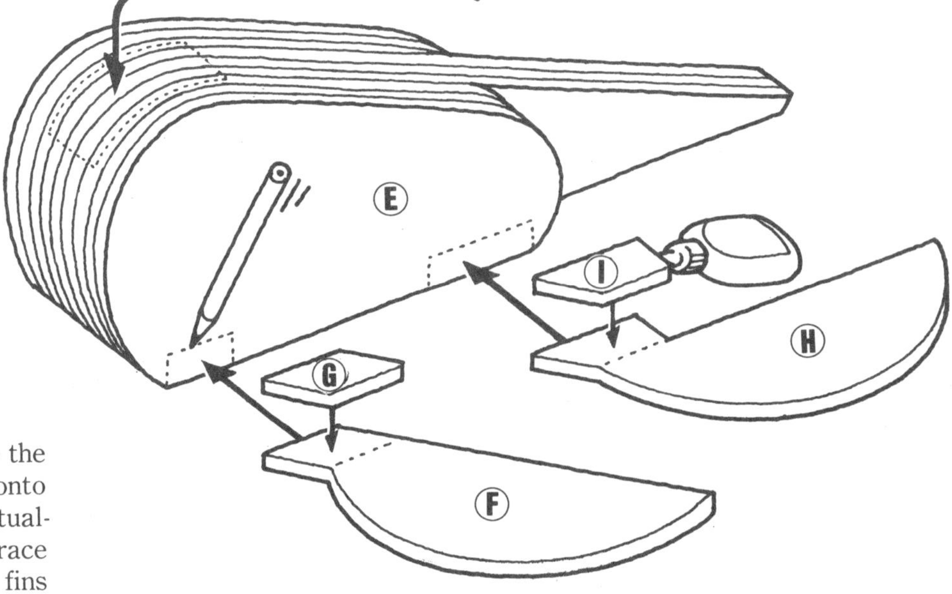

3

Next glue Ⓖ onto the fin Ⓕ, and Ⓘ onto fin Ⓗ. Use the actual-size drawing to trace the location of the fins and glue them into place. Lastly, connect the neck to the body.

FINISHED

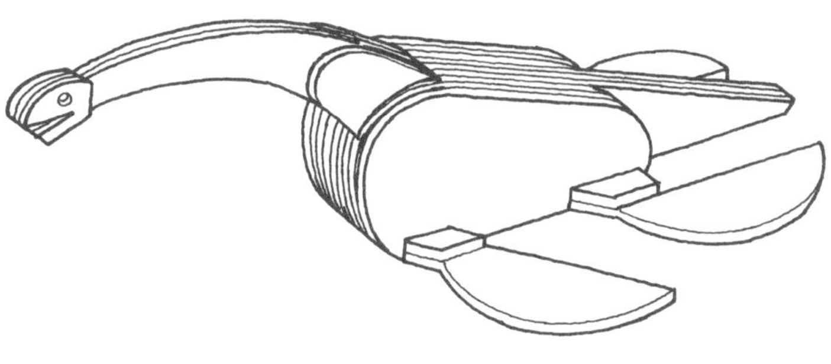

PTERANODON

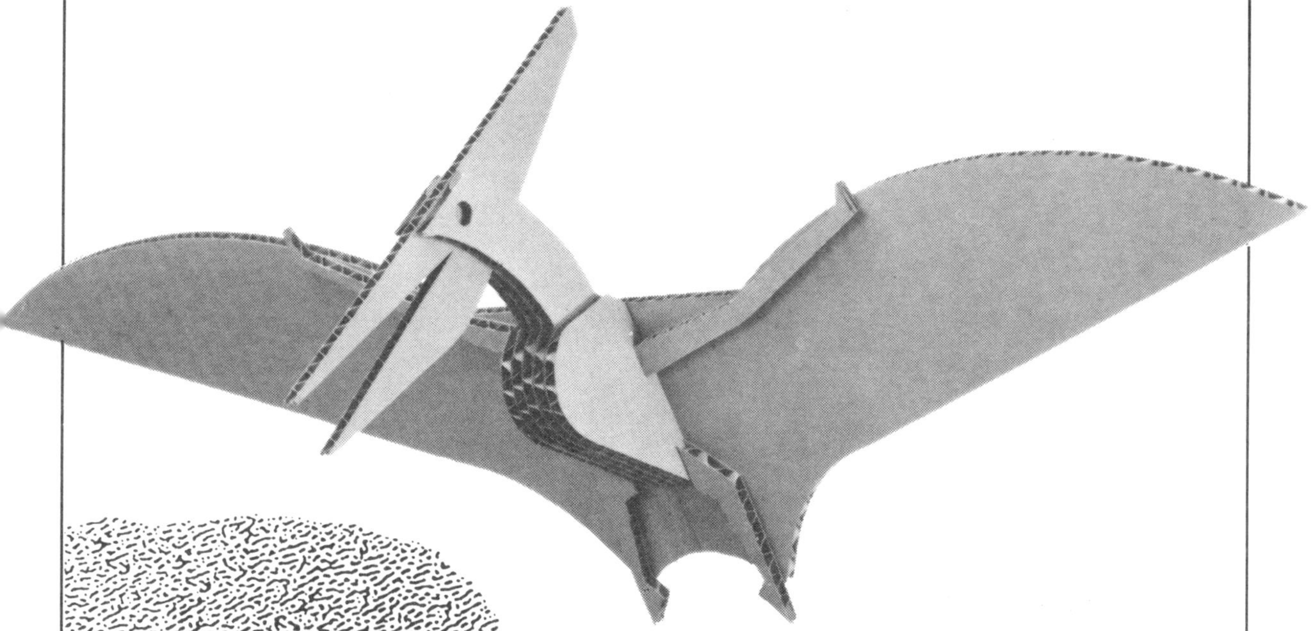

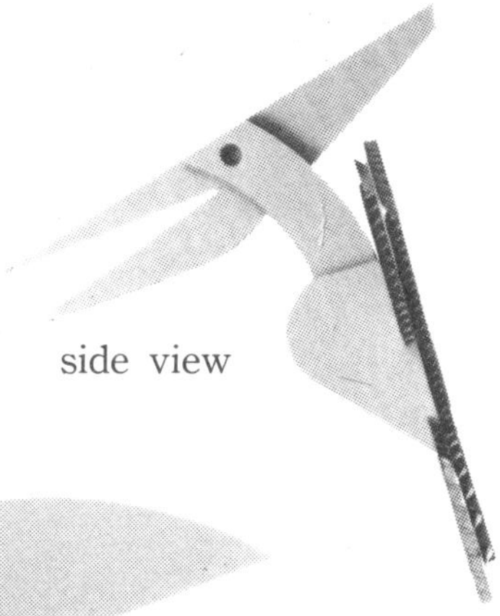

side view

view from above

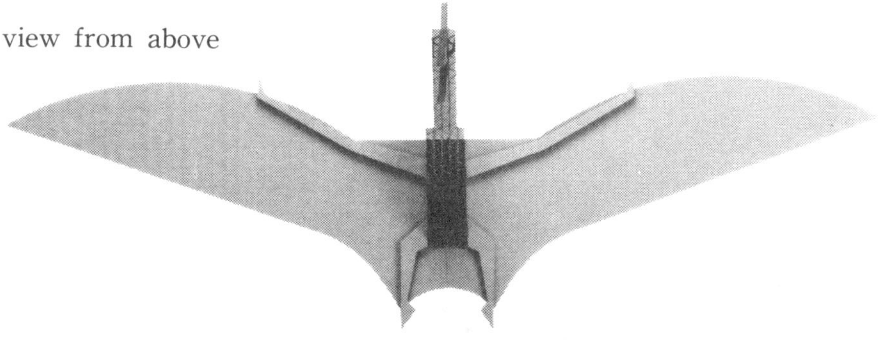

PTERANODON = ACTUAL-SIZE DRAWING〔 I 〕

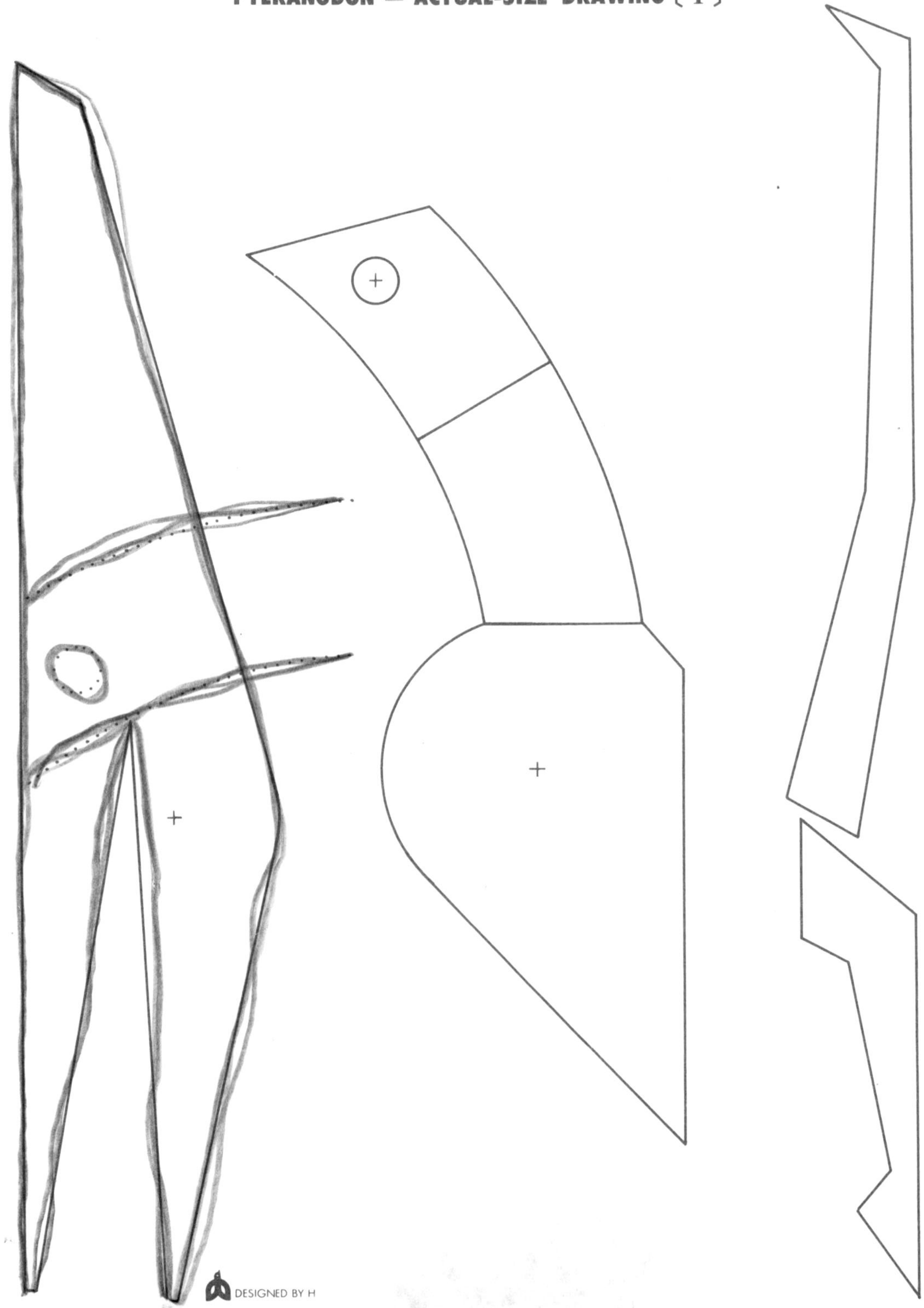

DESIGNED BY H

PTERANODON = ACTUAL-SIZE DRAWING〔II〕

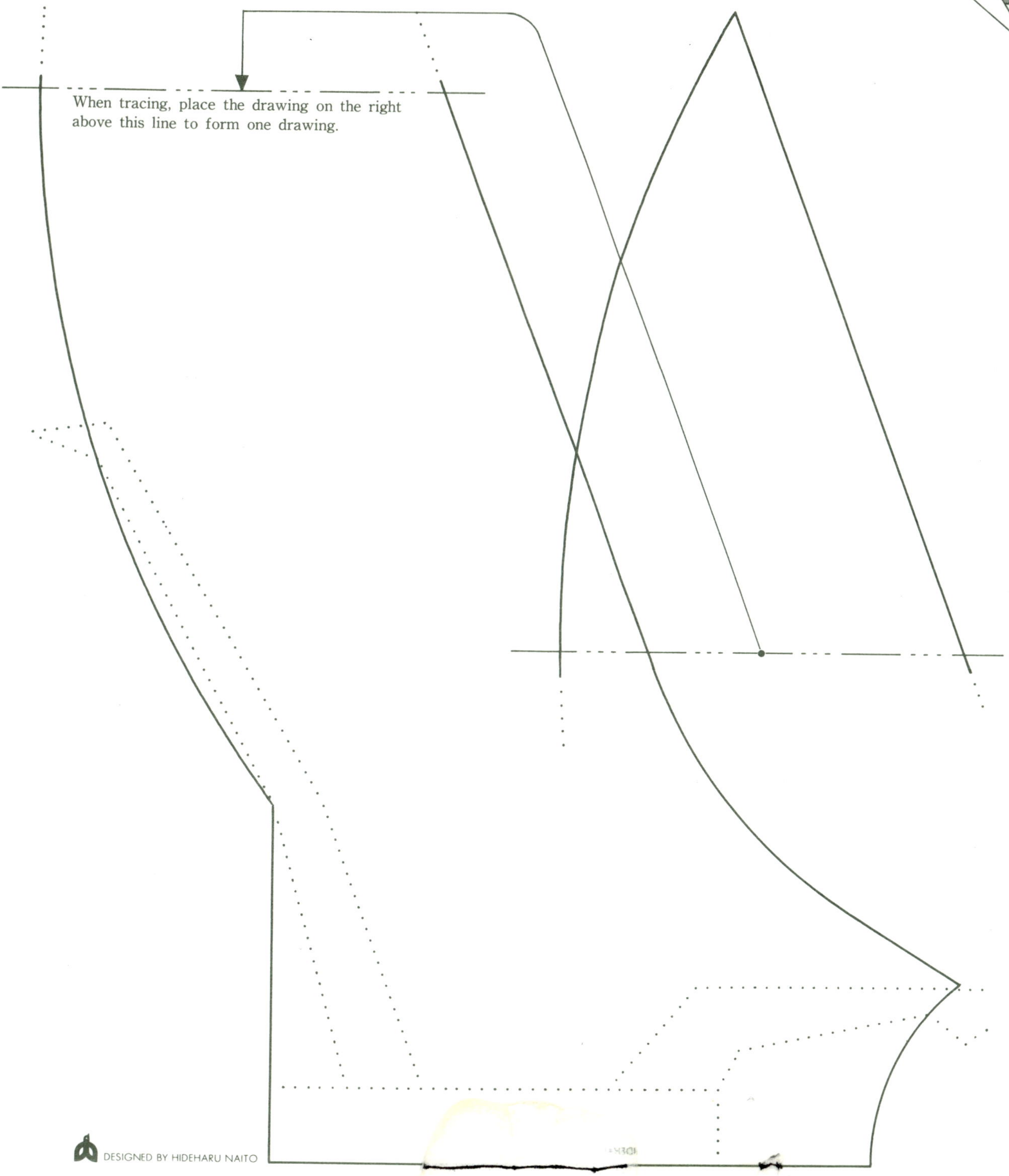

DESIGNED BY HIDEHARU NAITO

★ Double-check the number of parts

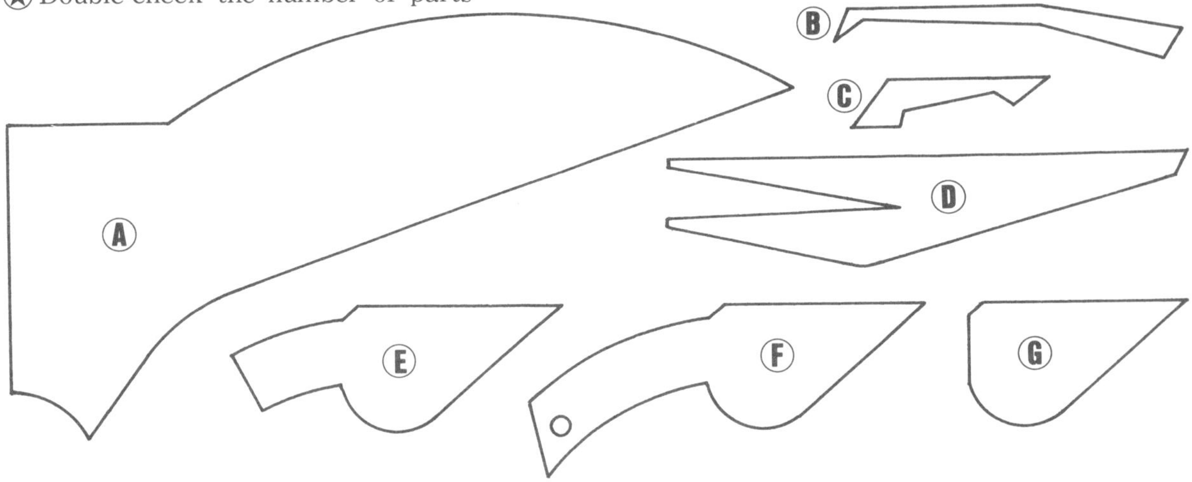

Ⓐ×2 Ⓑ×2 Ⓒ×2 Ⓓ×1
Ⓔ×1 Ⓕ×2 Ⓖ×2

1 As shown in the drawing, put the Ⓔ body part right in the middle, glue the Ⓕ parts on either side, and the Ⓖ parts on either side of that.

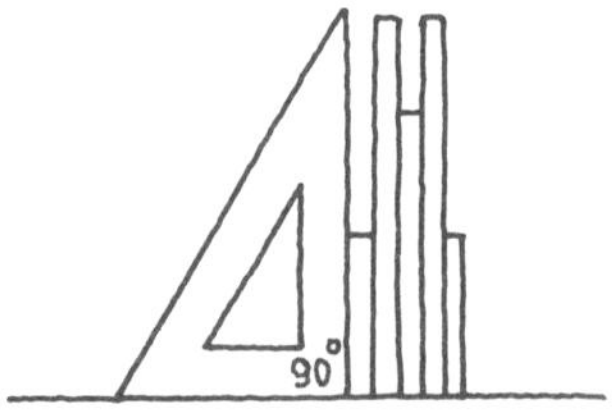

Use a triangle to ensure the torso is vertical.

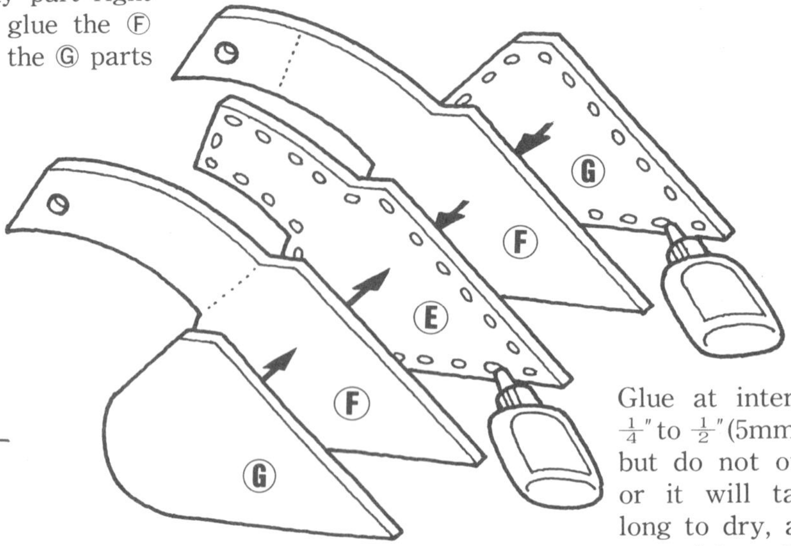

Glue at intervals of $\frac{1}{4}$" to $\frac{1}{2}$" (5mm–10mm), but do not overglue, or it will take too long to dry, and will not stick well.

2

Trace the location of the head Ⓕ on to the beak Ⓓ.

Next, apply glue to the beak as shown, but dab only a little bit where the star is.

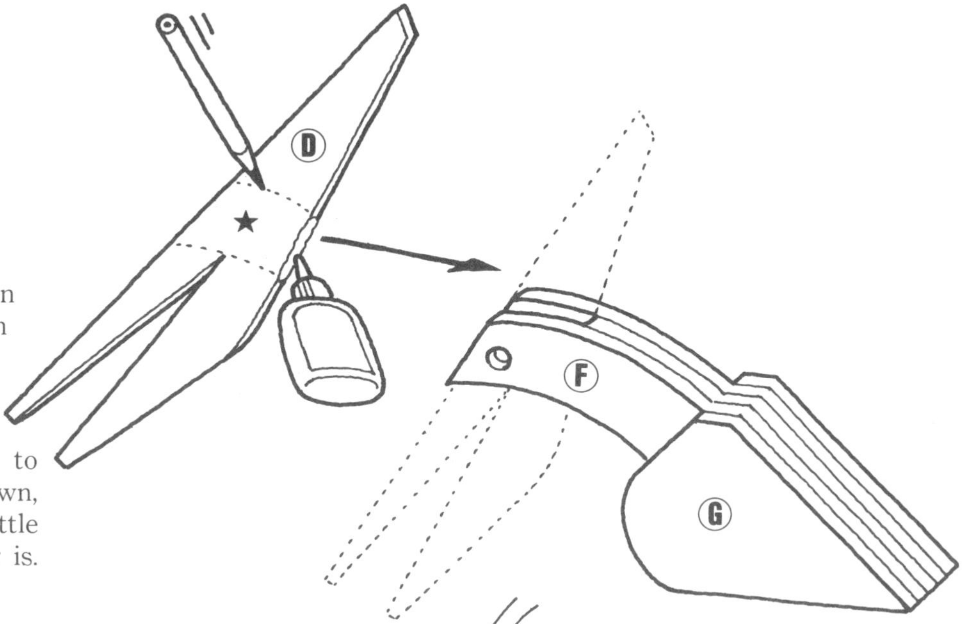

Insert the beak Ⓓ into the head Ⓕ.

3

Attach the wings to each other as shown. Trace onto the wings the location of the torso. Glue the back of the torso (straight part) onto the wings.

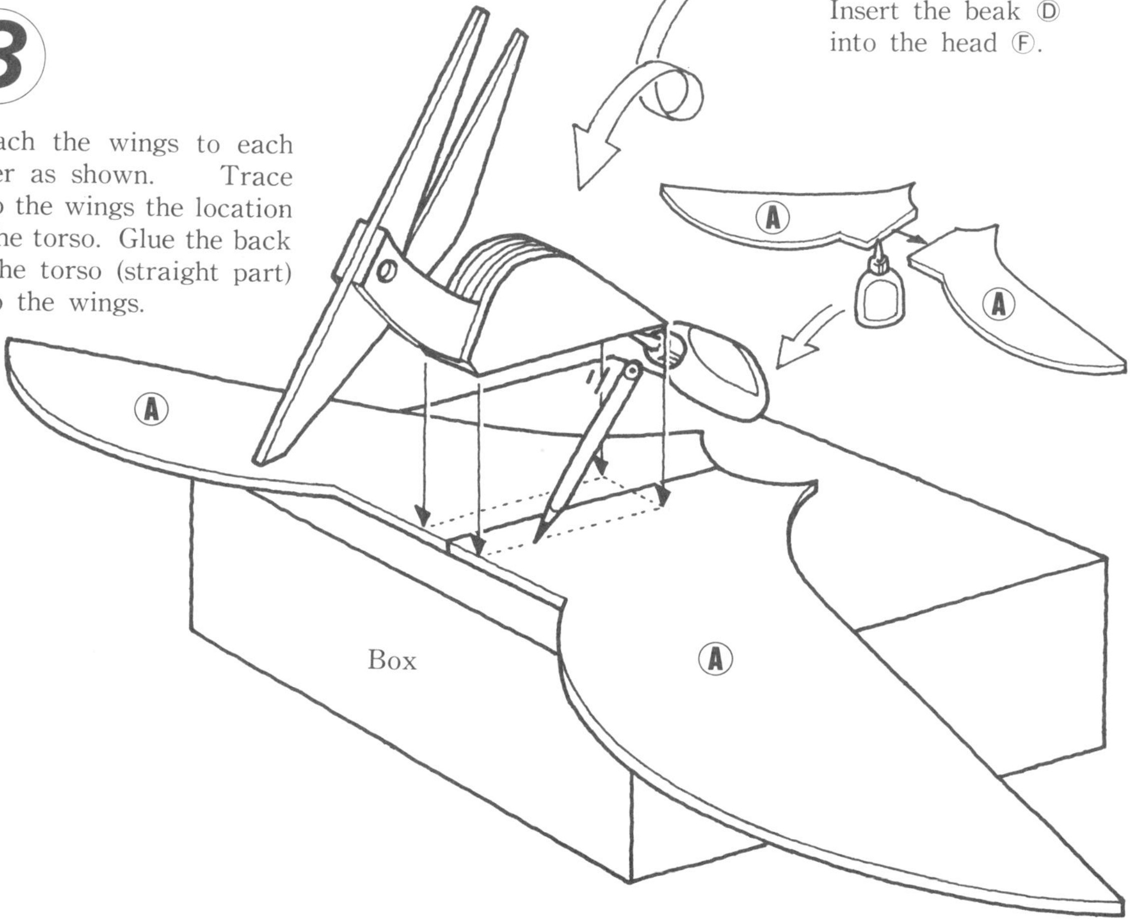

4

Trace the location of the arms Ⓑ and legs Ⓒ onto the wings. Apply glue to the arms and legs and attach them to the wings.

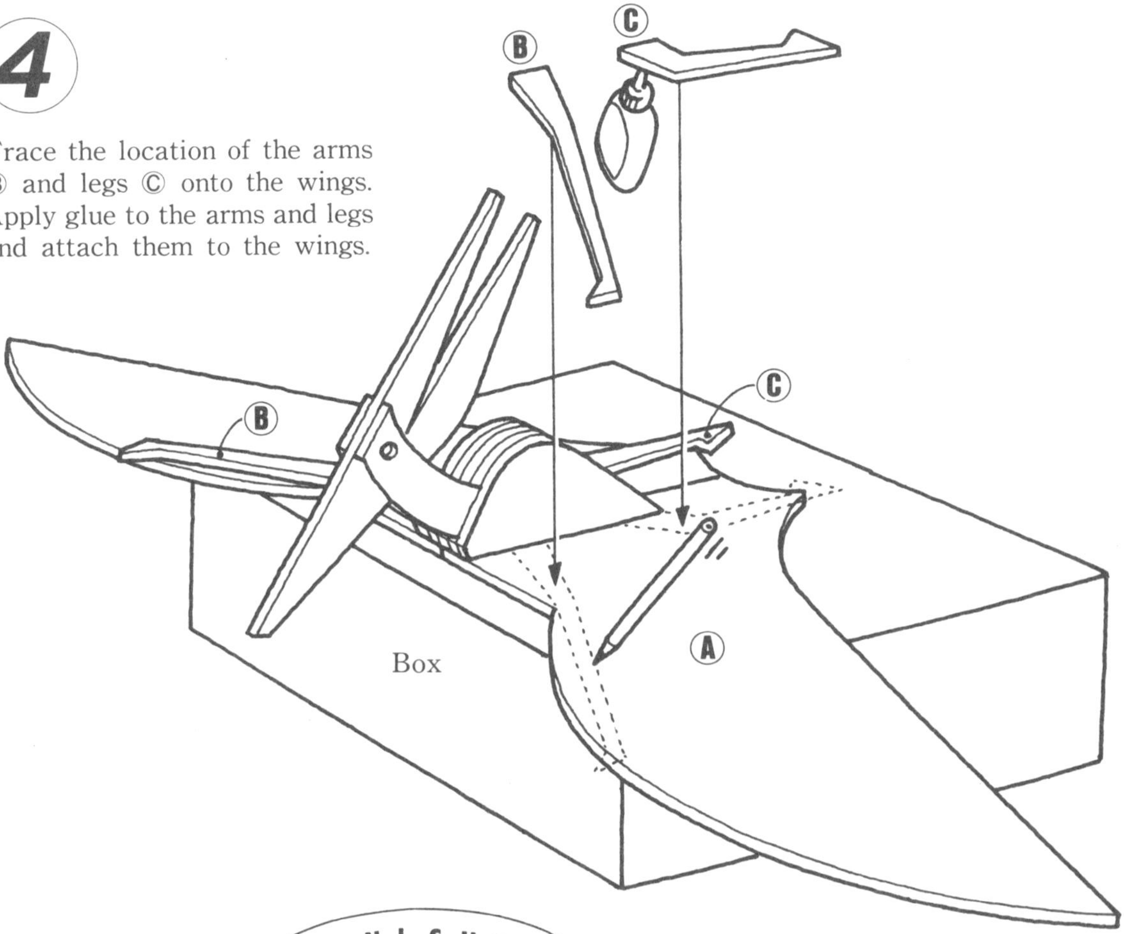

FINISHED

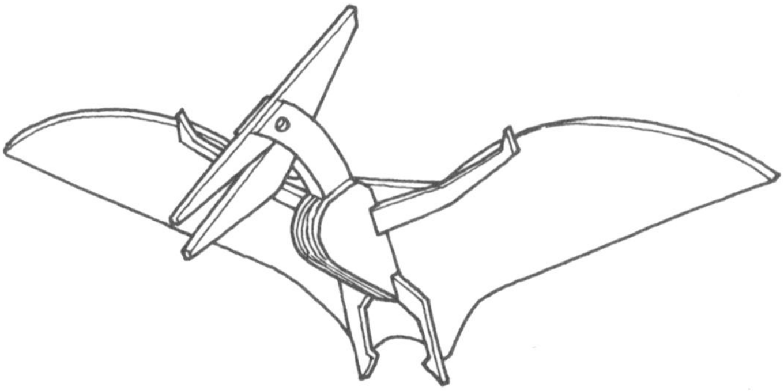

PARASAUROLOPHUS

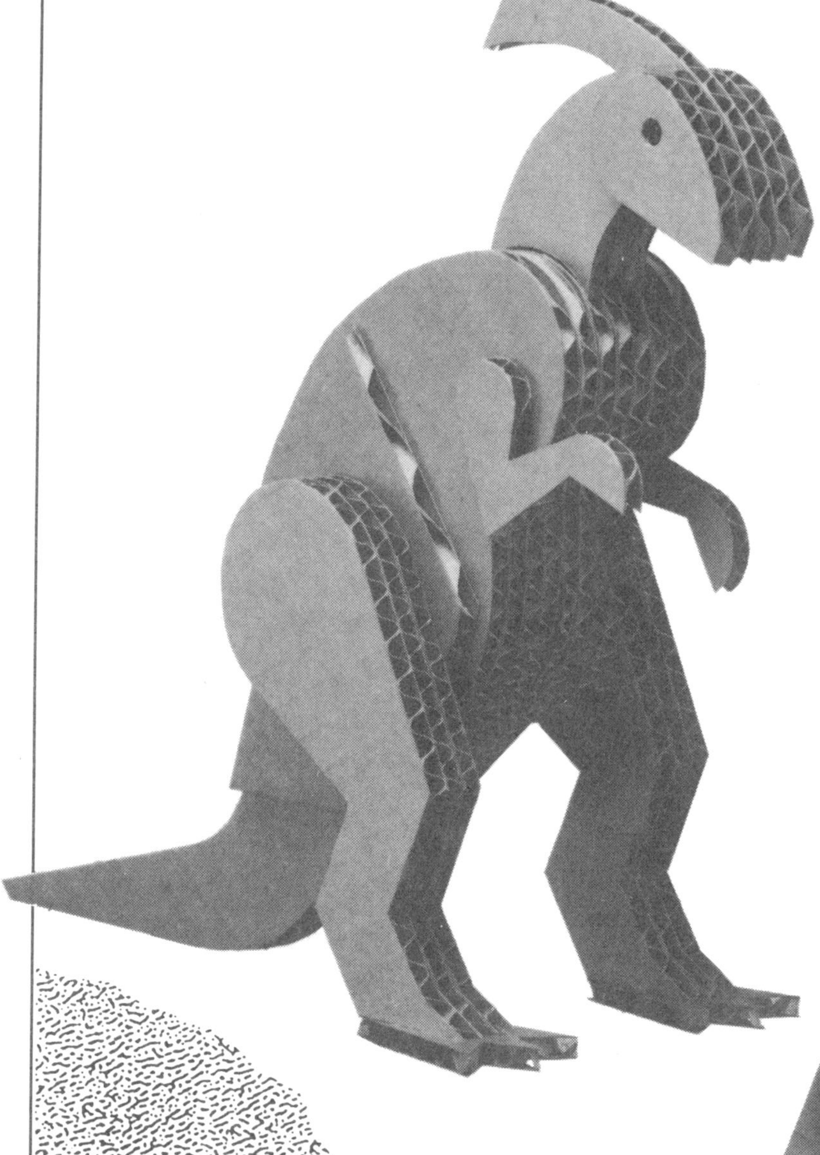

front view

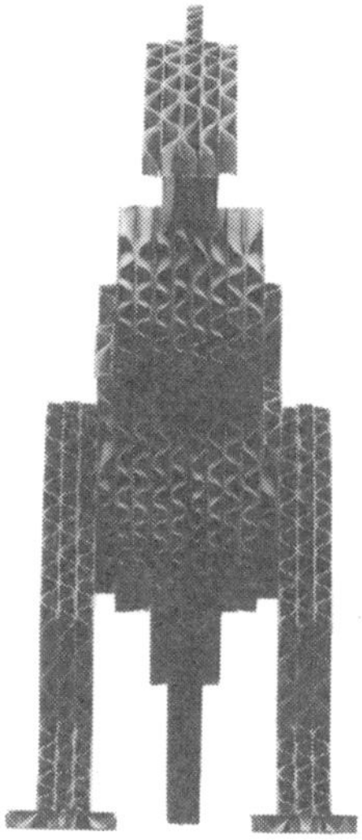

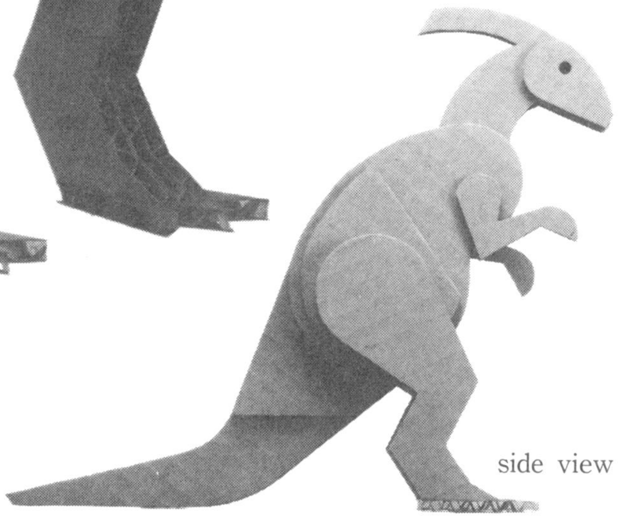

side view

PARASAUROLOPHUS = ACTUAL-SIZE DRAWING〔 I 〕

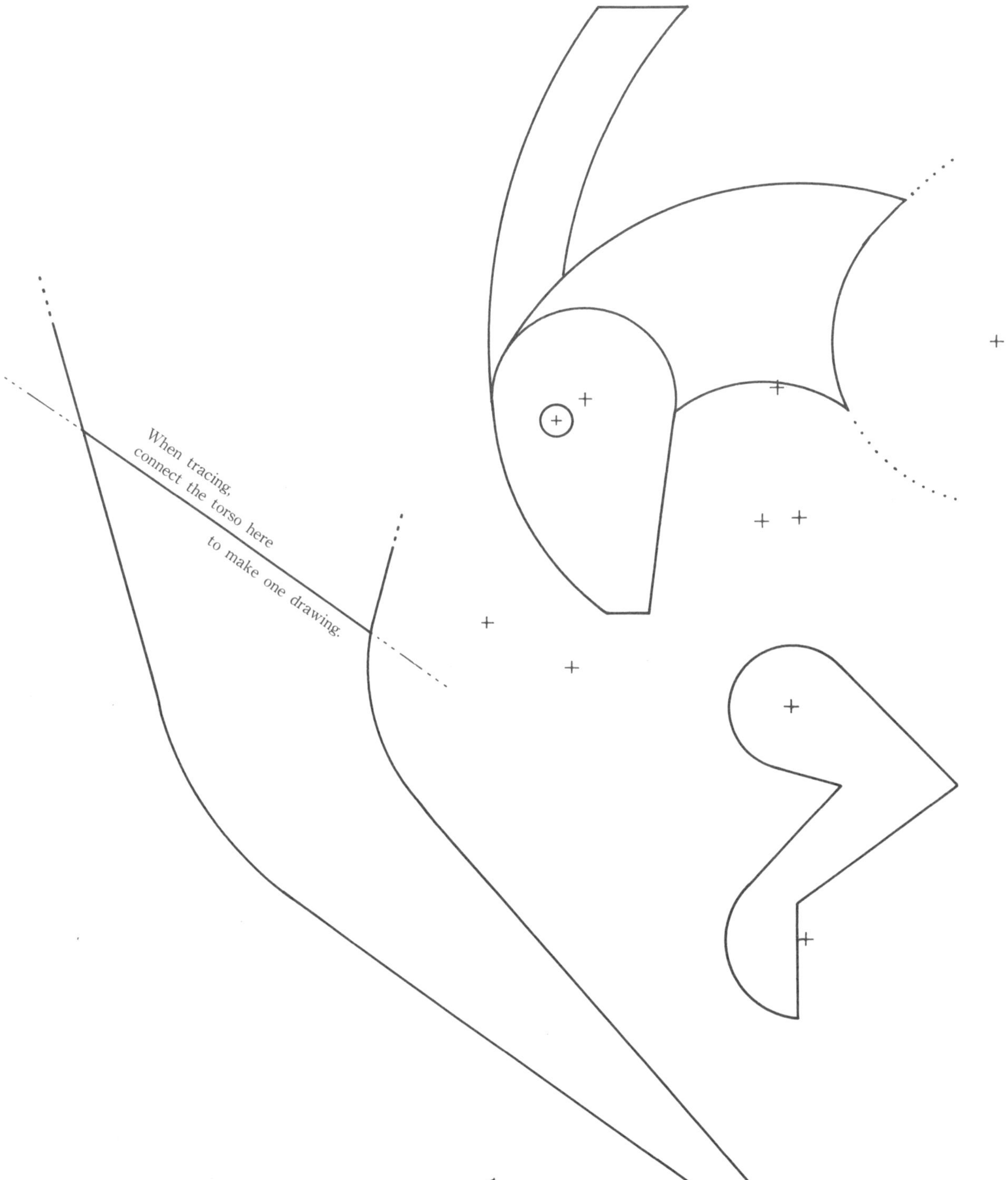

DESIGNED BY HIDEHARU NAITO

PARASAUROLOPHUS = ACTUAL-SIZE DRAWING〔II〕

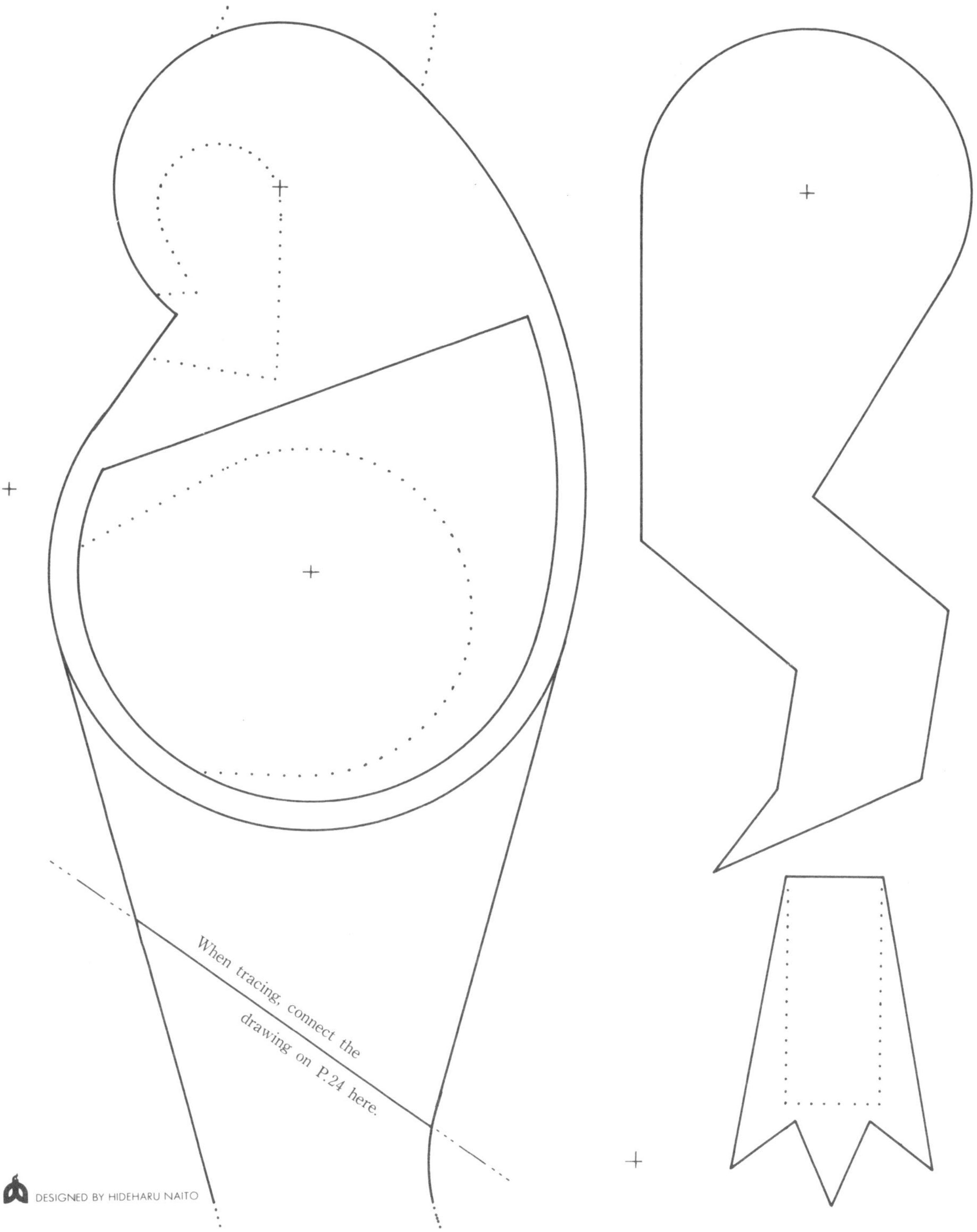

DESIGNED BY HIDEHARU NAITO

★ Double-check the number of parts

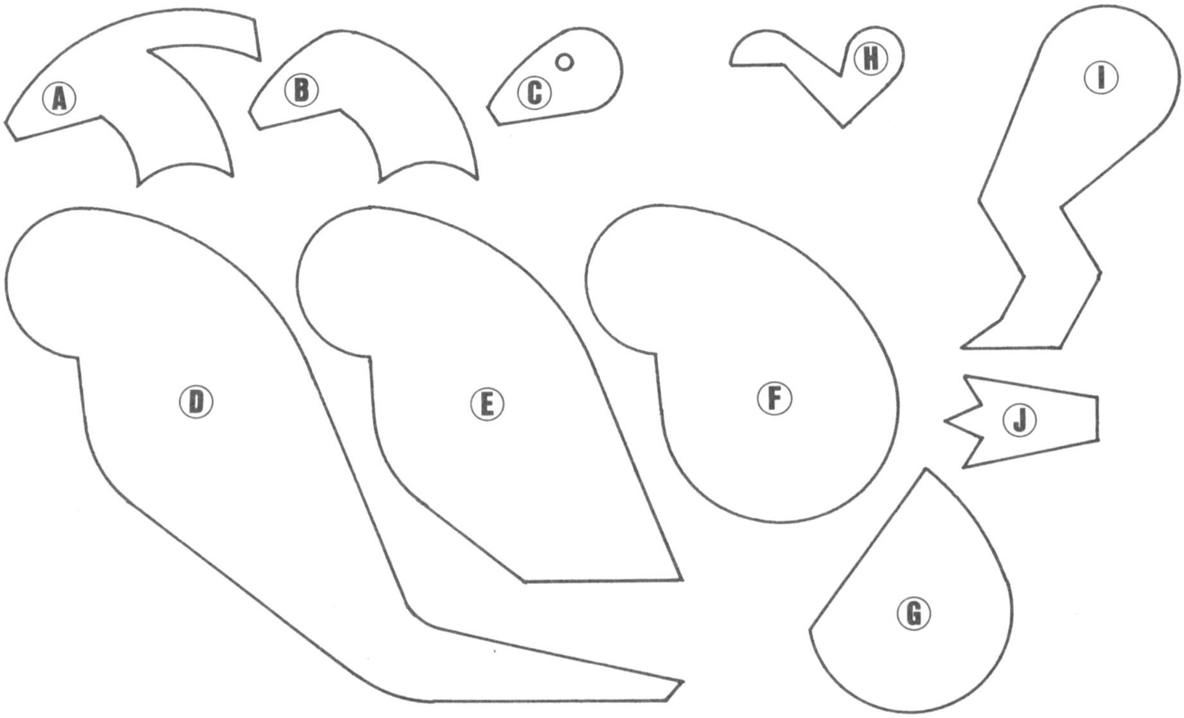

Ⓐ×1 Ⓑ×2 Ⓒ×2 Ⓓ×2 Ⓔ×2
Ⓕ×4 Ⓖ×2 Ⓗ×2 Ⓘ×6 Ⓙ×2

1

To make the head, put Ⓐ in the middle, glue Ⓑs on either side, then glue Ⓒs on either side of that.

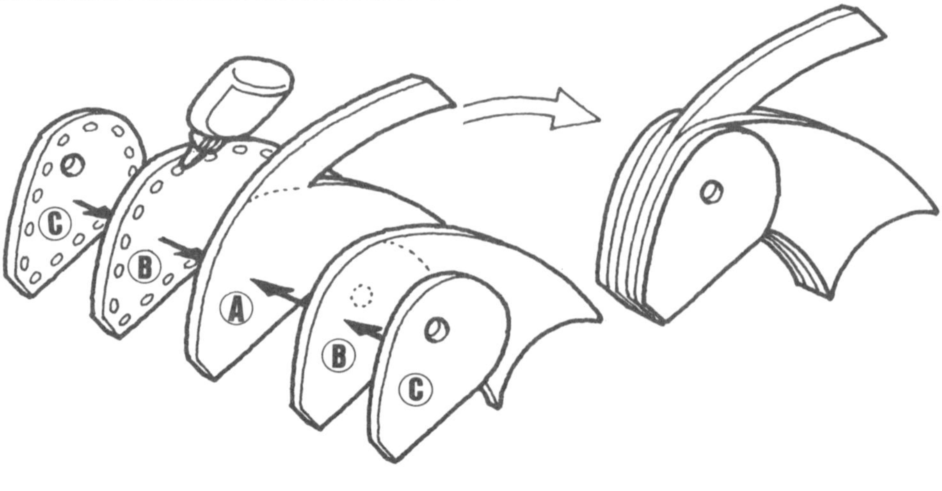

2

For the torso, glue the 2 Ⓓ parts together. Glue an Ⓔ piece on either side of the Ⓓs. Add 2 Ⓕ pieces on each side, (4 total). Then, as shown, glue the Ⓖ parts onto the Ⓕ parts.

N.B: Use a triangle to make everything vertical, and trace the location of the Ⓖ parts before gluing.

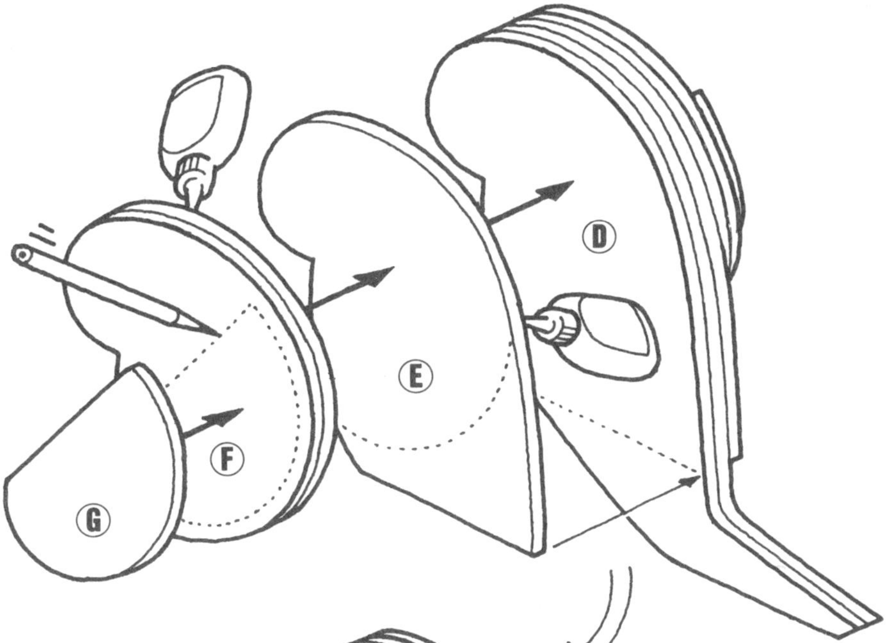

3

As shown, glue the legs, Ⓘ, onto the feet, Ⓙ. Next, use the actual-size drawing to trace the location of the legs and glue onto Ⓖ.

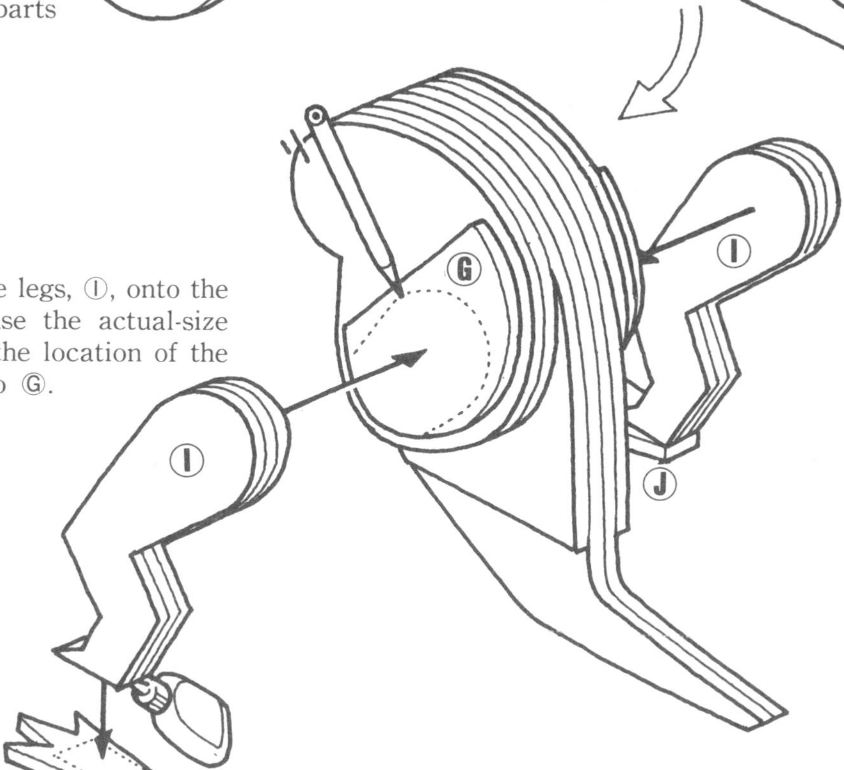

4

As shown, glue the head and front legs onto the torso.

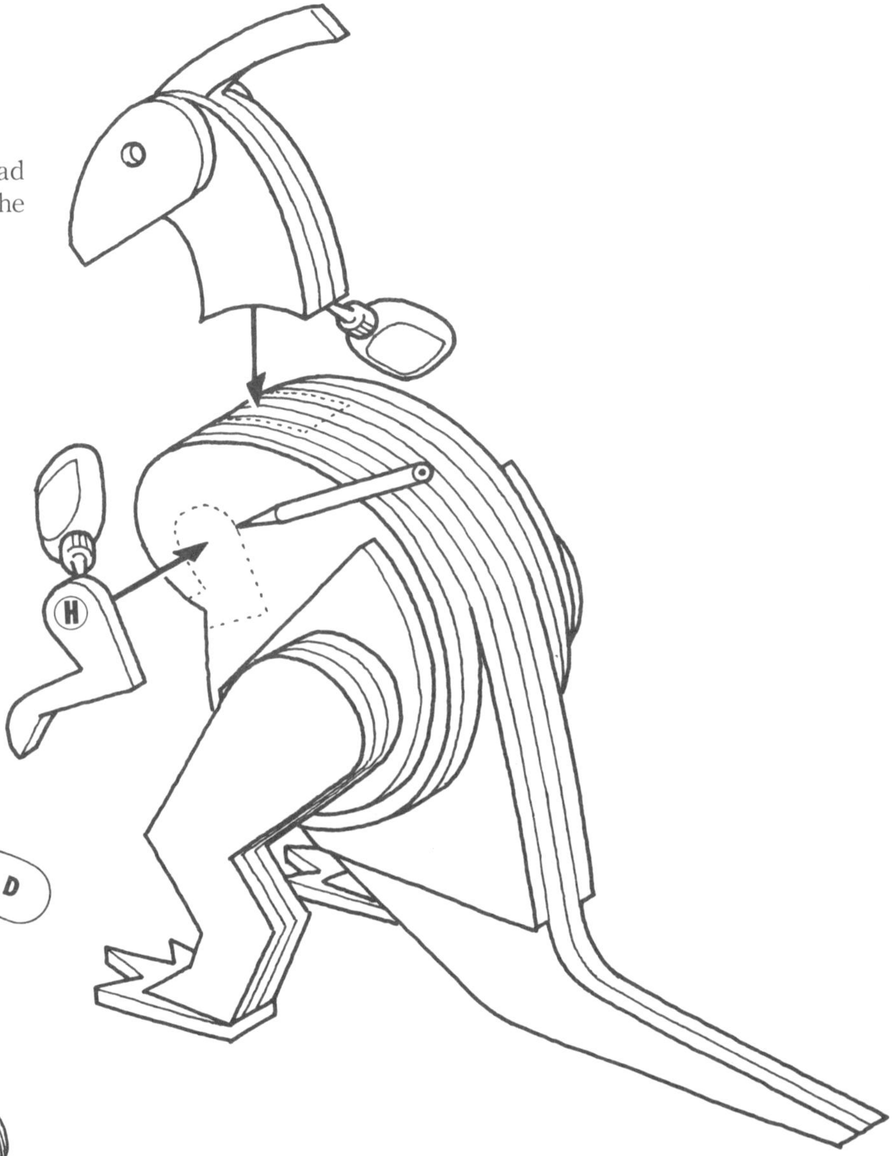

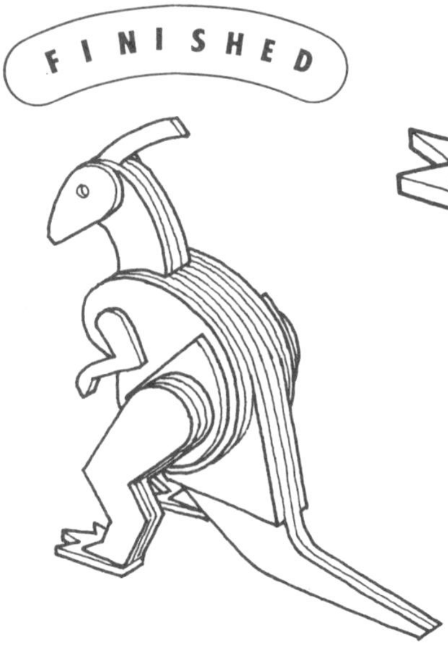

SCOLOSAURUS

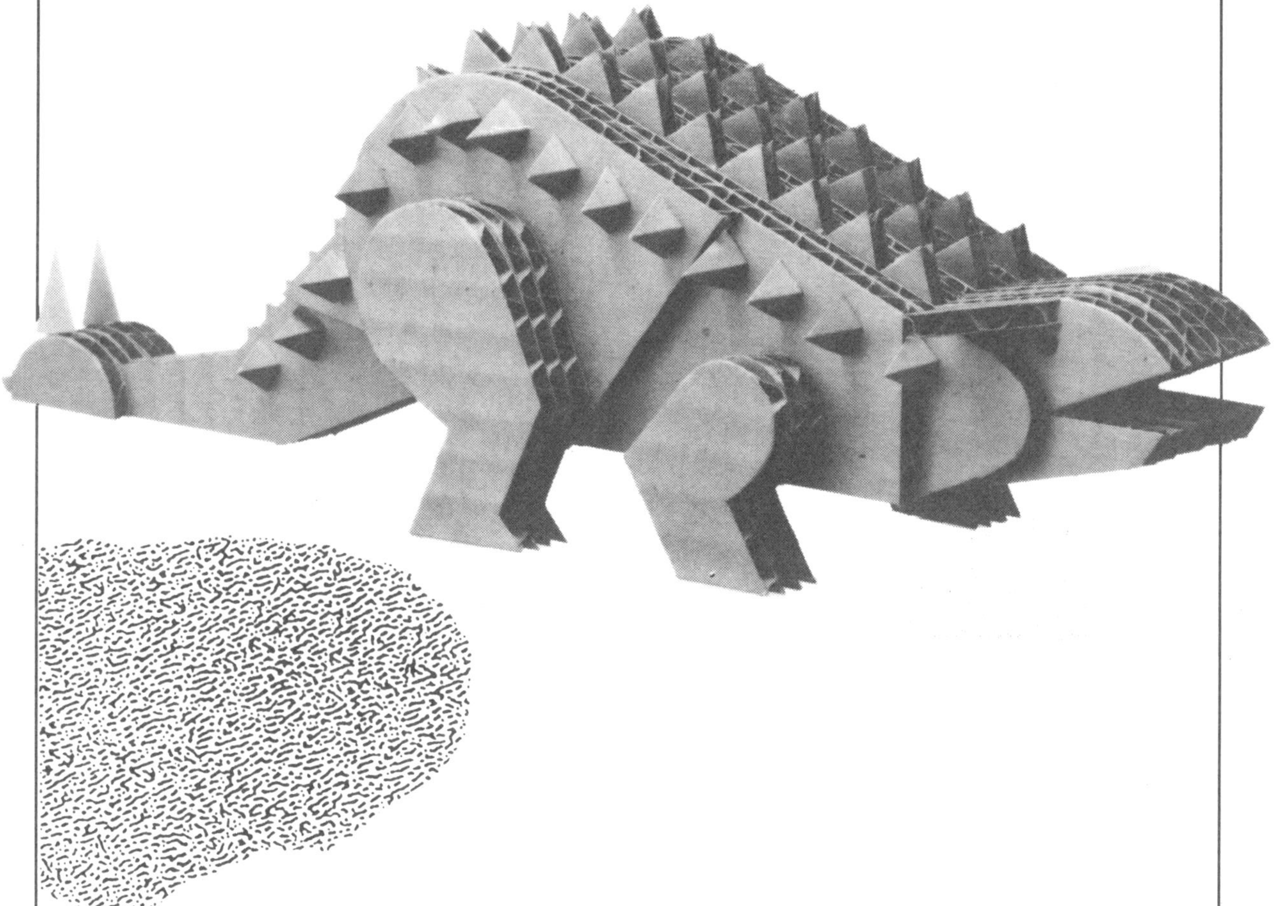

side view

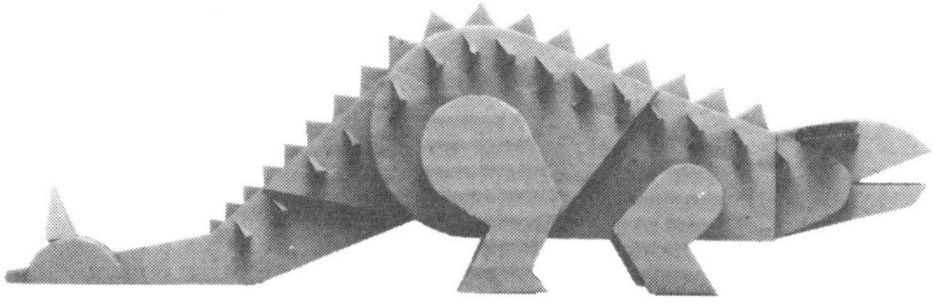

front view

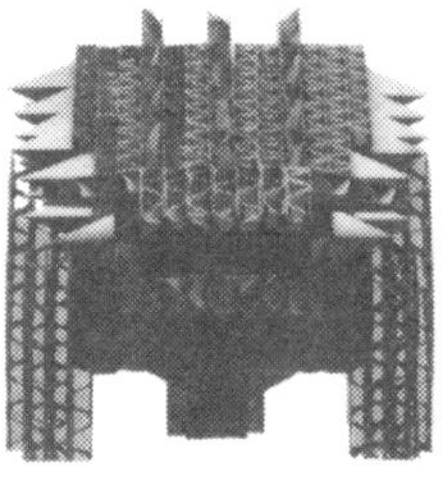

SCOLOSAURUS = ACTUAL-SIZE DRAWING〔 I 〕

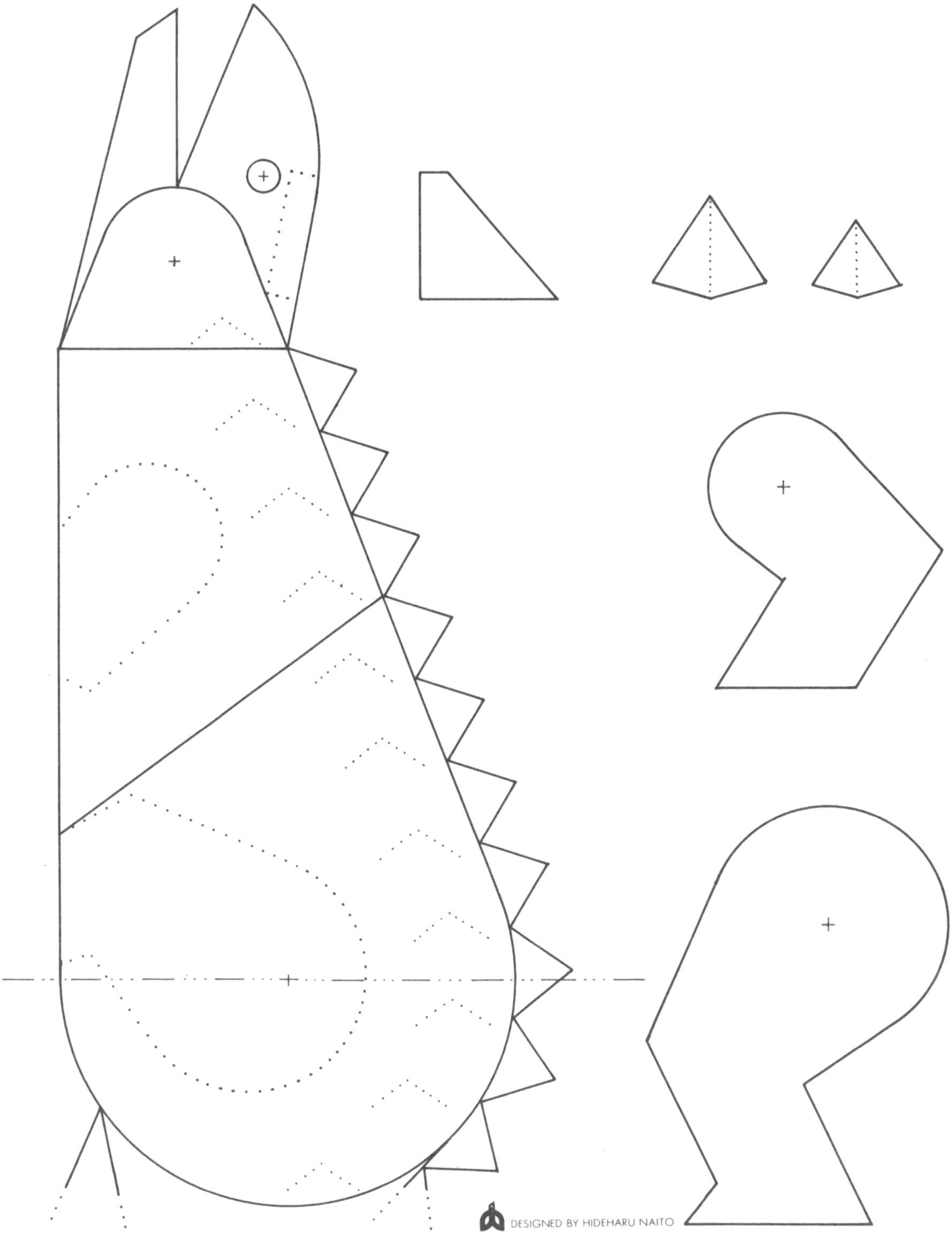

DESIGNED BY HIDEHARU NAITO

SCOLOSAURUS = ACTUAL-SIZE DRAWING〔II〕

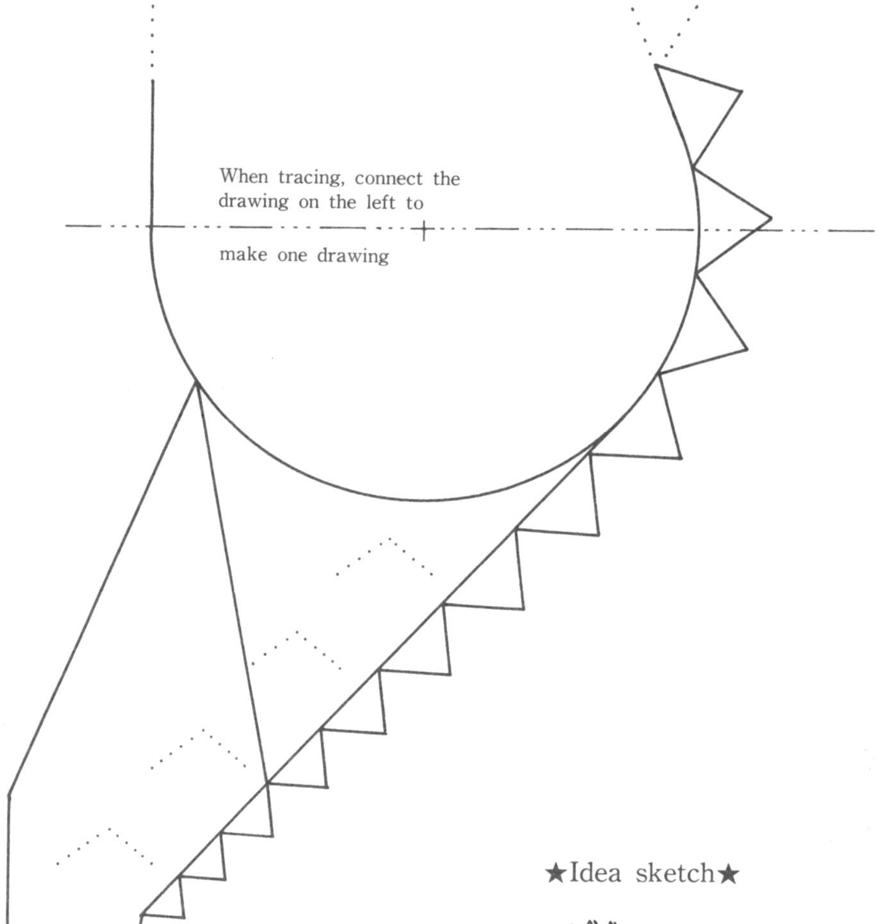

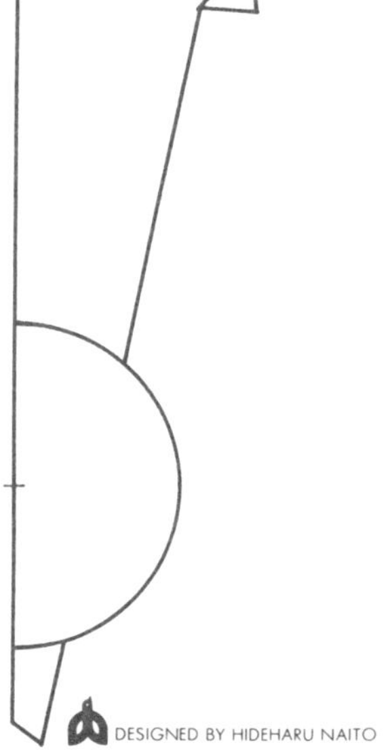

★Idea sketch★

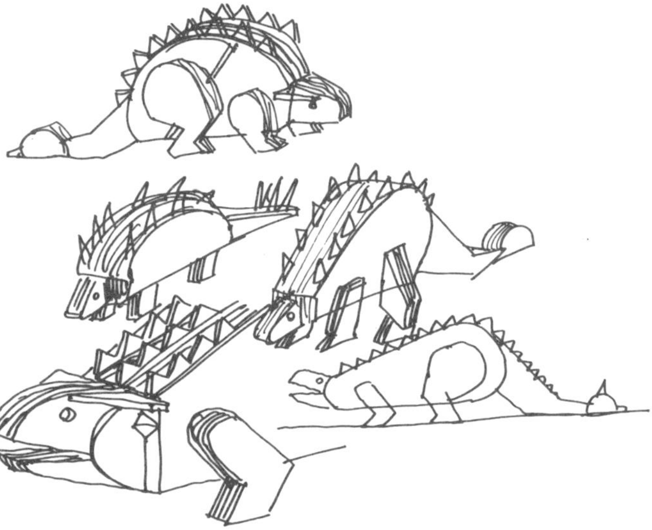

DESIGNED BY HIDEHARU NAITO

SCOLOSAURUS = ASSEMBLY INSTRUCTIONS

★ Double-check the number of parts

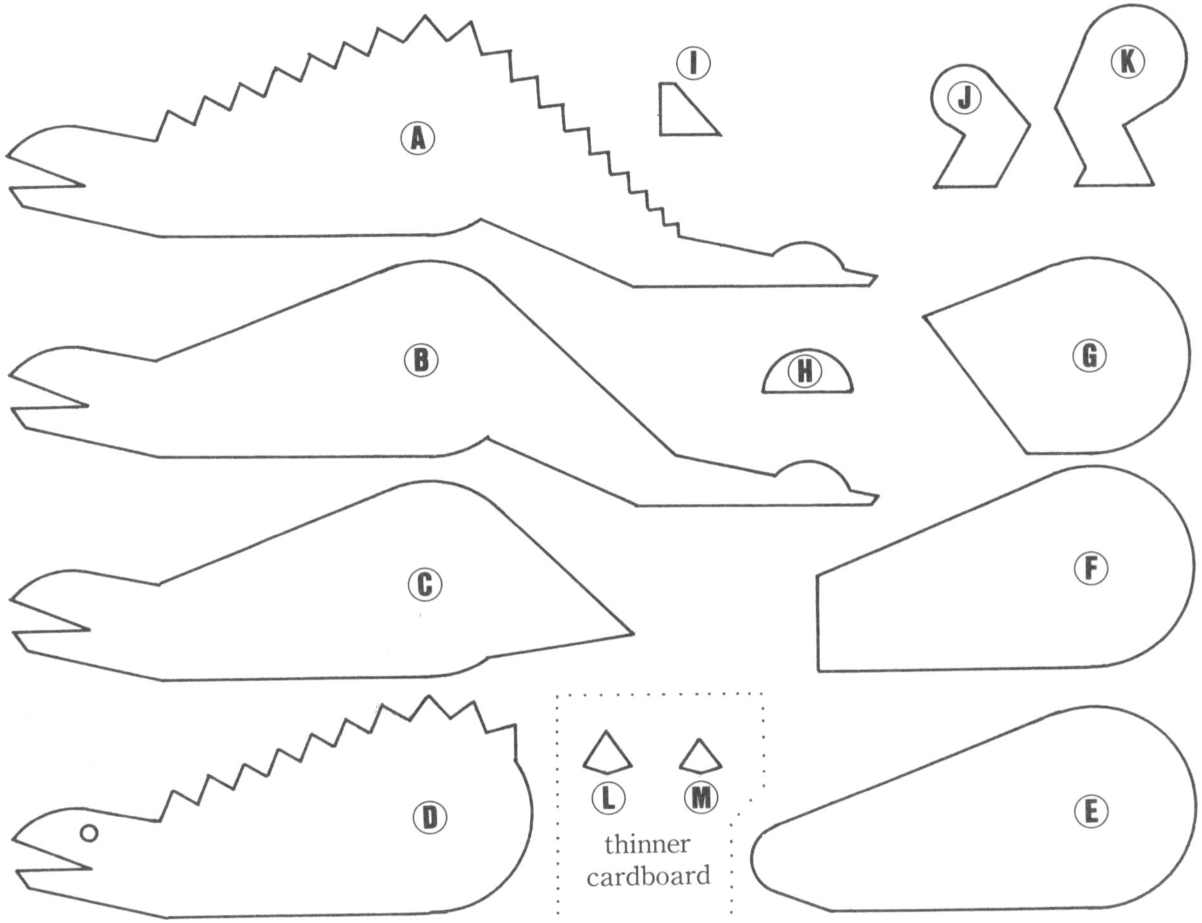

Ⓐ×1 Ⓑ×2 Ⓒ×2 Ⓓ×2
Ⓔ×2 Ⓕ×2 Ⓖ×2 Ⓗ×2
Ⓘ×2 Ⓙ×6 Ⓚ×6
Ⓛ×2 (thinner cardboard)
Ⓜ×30 (thinner cardboard)

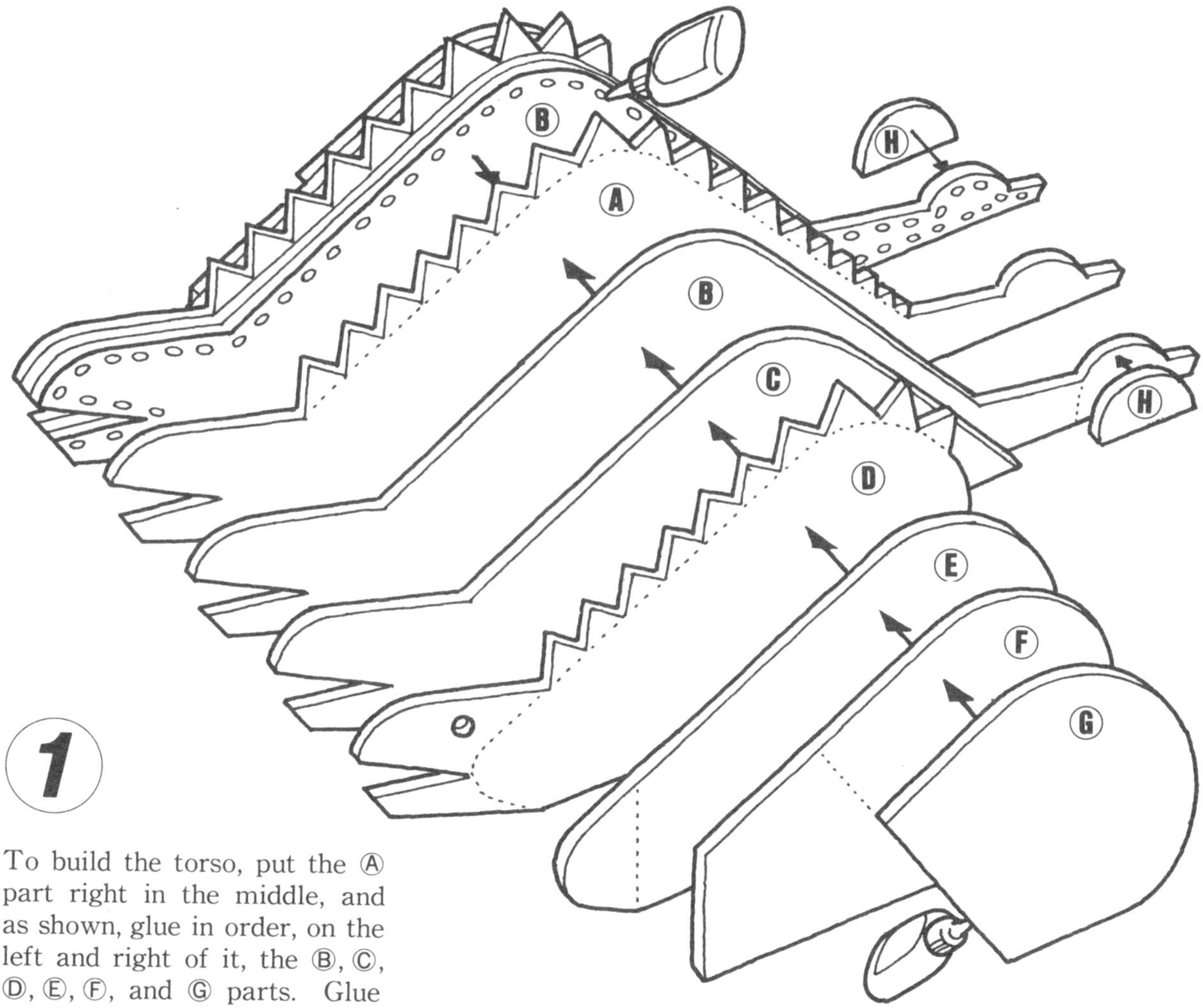

1

To build the torso, put the Ⓐ part right in the middle, and as shown, glue in order, on the left and right of it, the Ⓑ, Ⓒ, Ⓓ, Ⓔ, Ⓕ, and Ⓖ parts. Glue on the tail parts Ⓗ as shown.

Dab the glue around the edges at intervals of $\frac{1}{4}''$ to $\frac{1}{2}''$ (5mm-10mm), and use a triangle to make sure the parts are perfectly vertical.

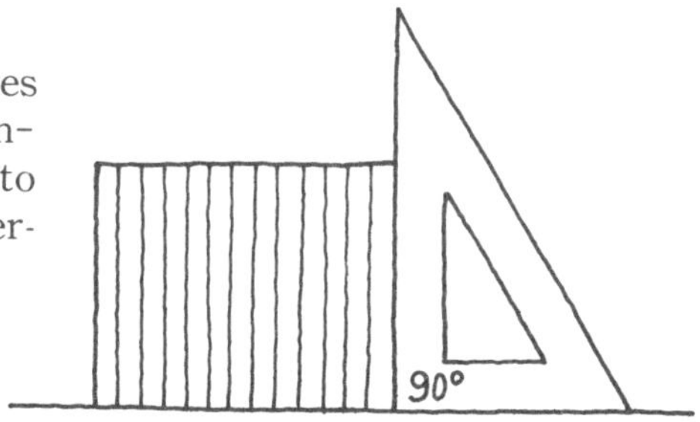

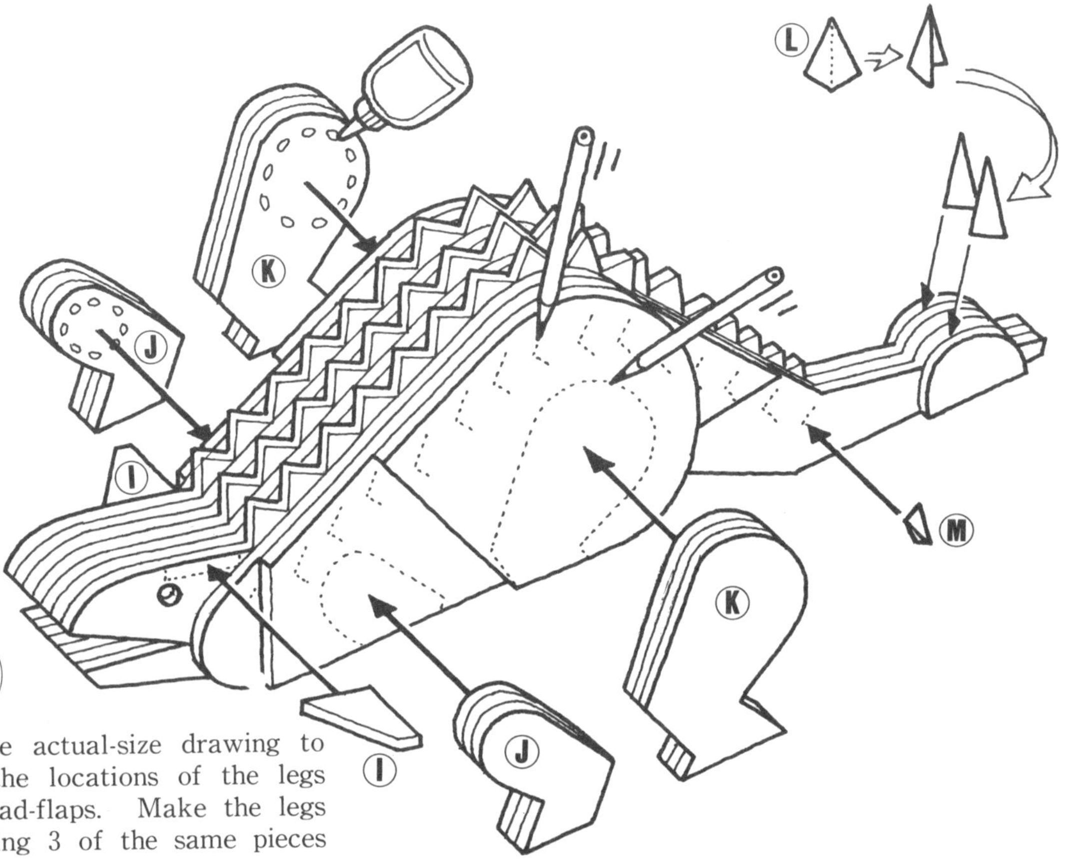

2

Use the actual-size drawing to trace the locations of the legs and head-flaps. Make the legs by gluing 3 of the same pieces together.
Glue on the flaps Ⓘ and legs Ⓙ and Ⓚ. Fold the Ⓛ and Ⓜ parts as shown and glue on.
(See photograph)

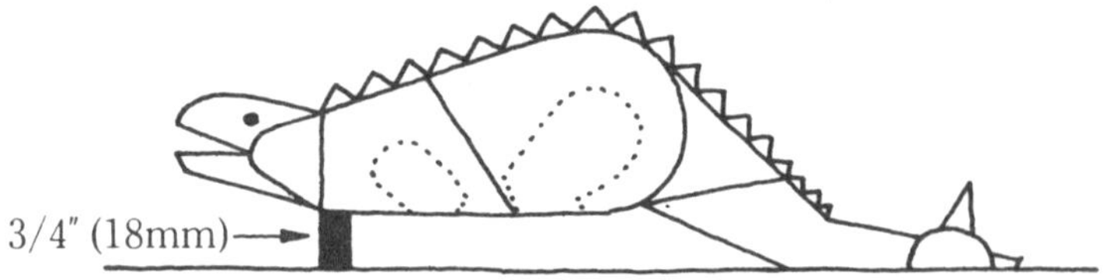

N.B: When gluing the legs on, support the front of the torso with a block of cardboard about 3/4″ (18mm) high.

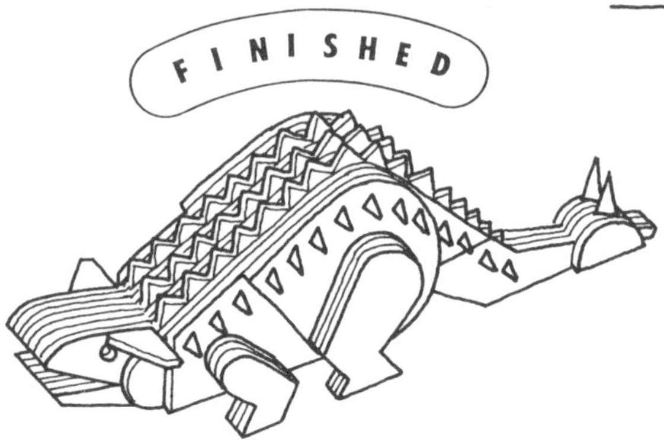

TRICERATOPS

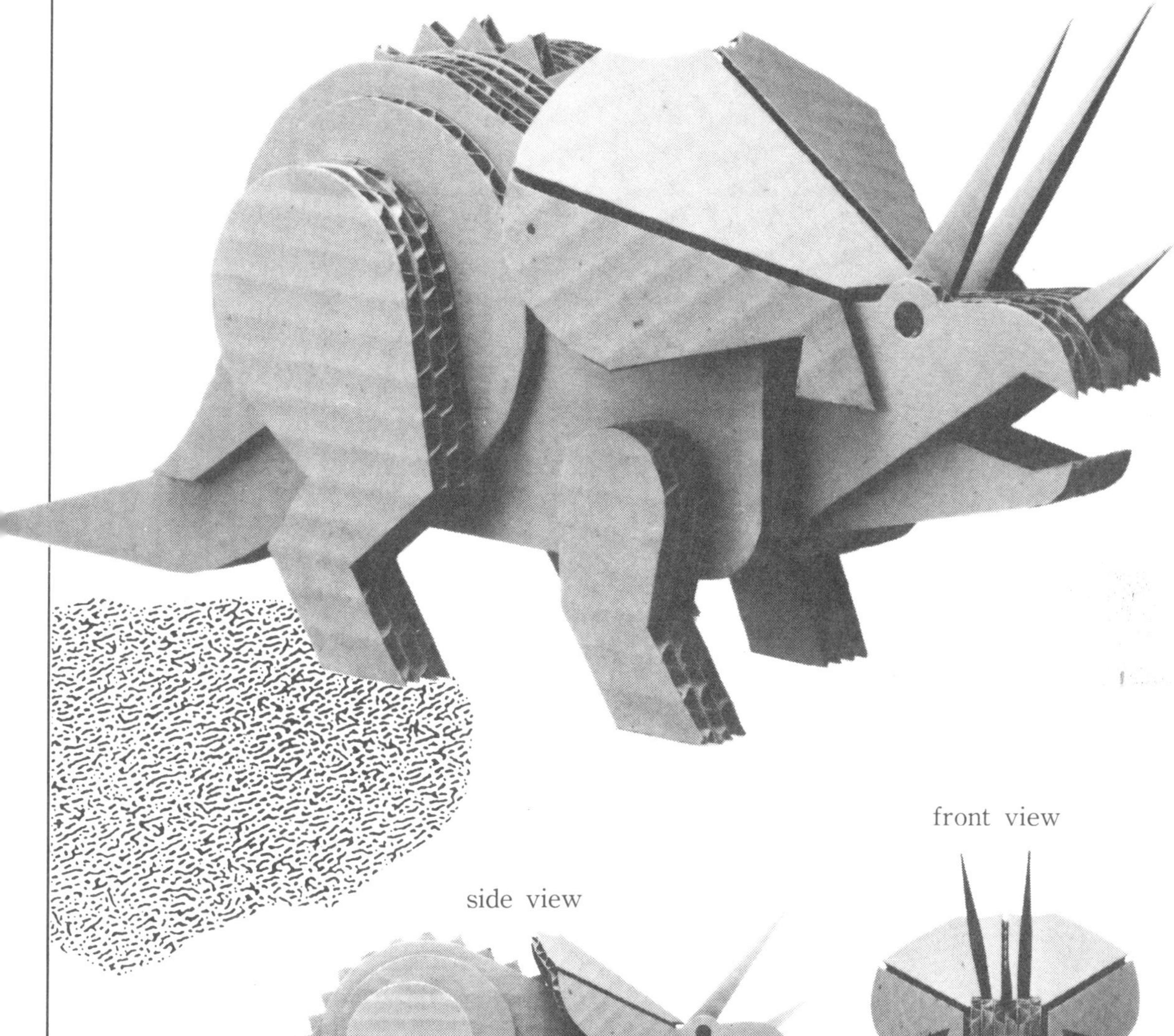

front view

side view

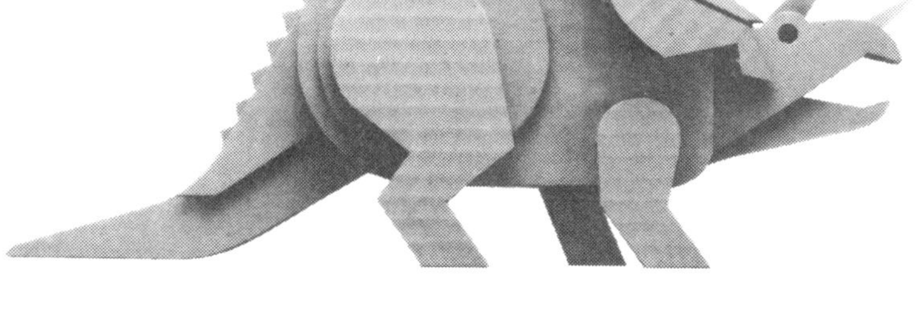

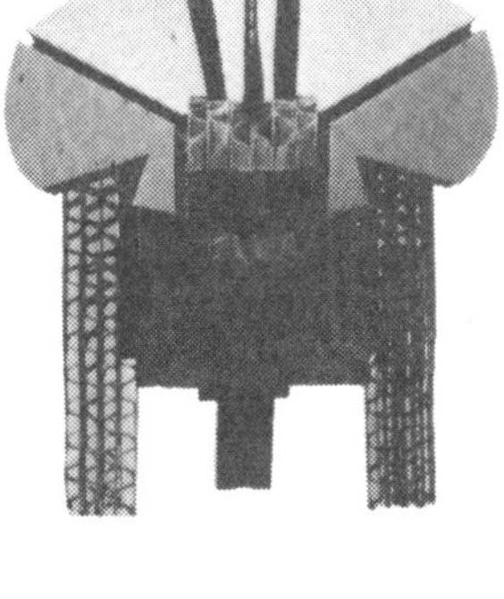

TRICERATOPS = ACTUAL-SIZE DRAWING〔 I 〕

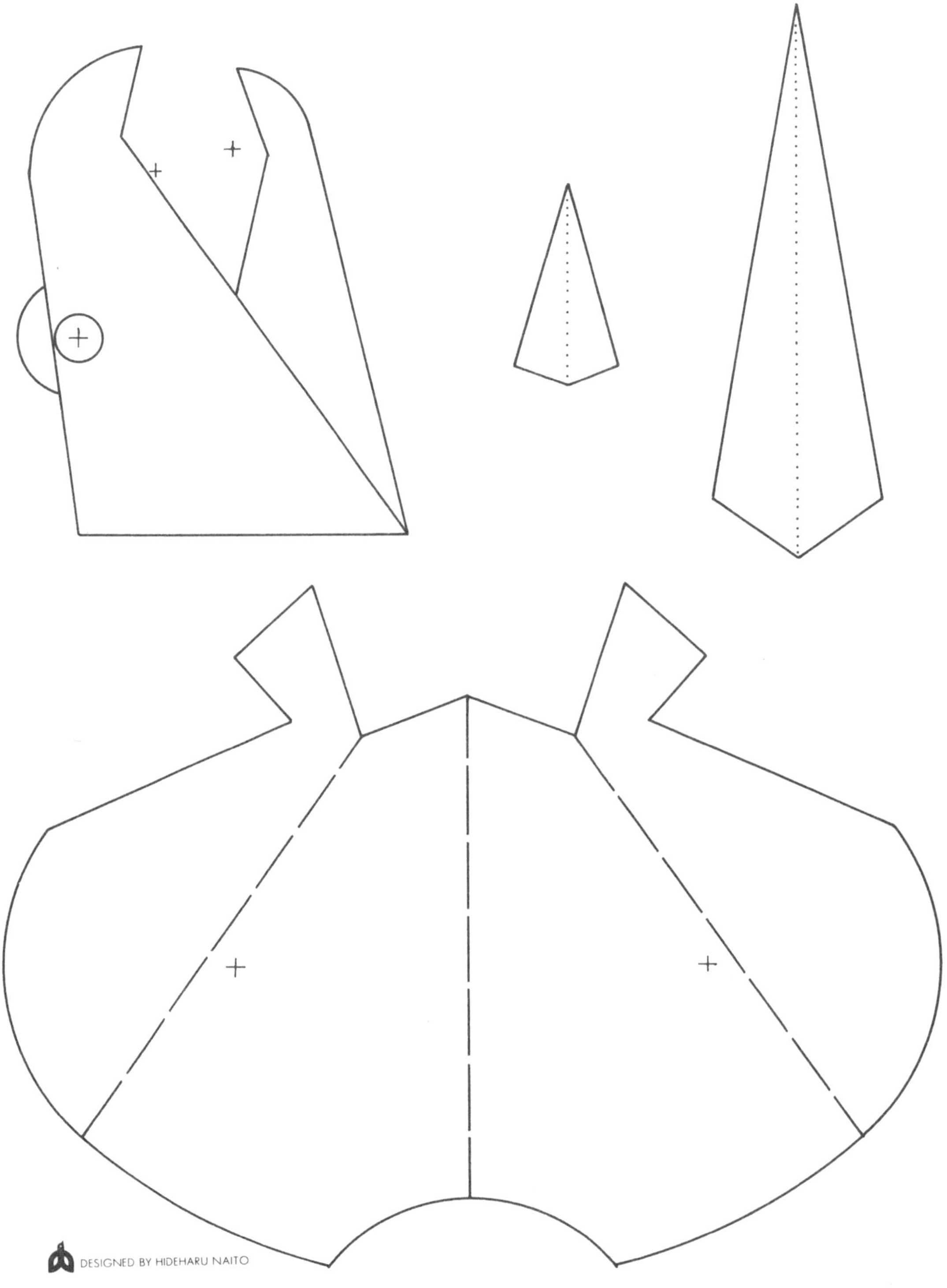

DESIGNED BY HIDEHARU NAITO

TRICERATOPS = ACTUAL-SIZE DRAWING〔II〕

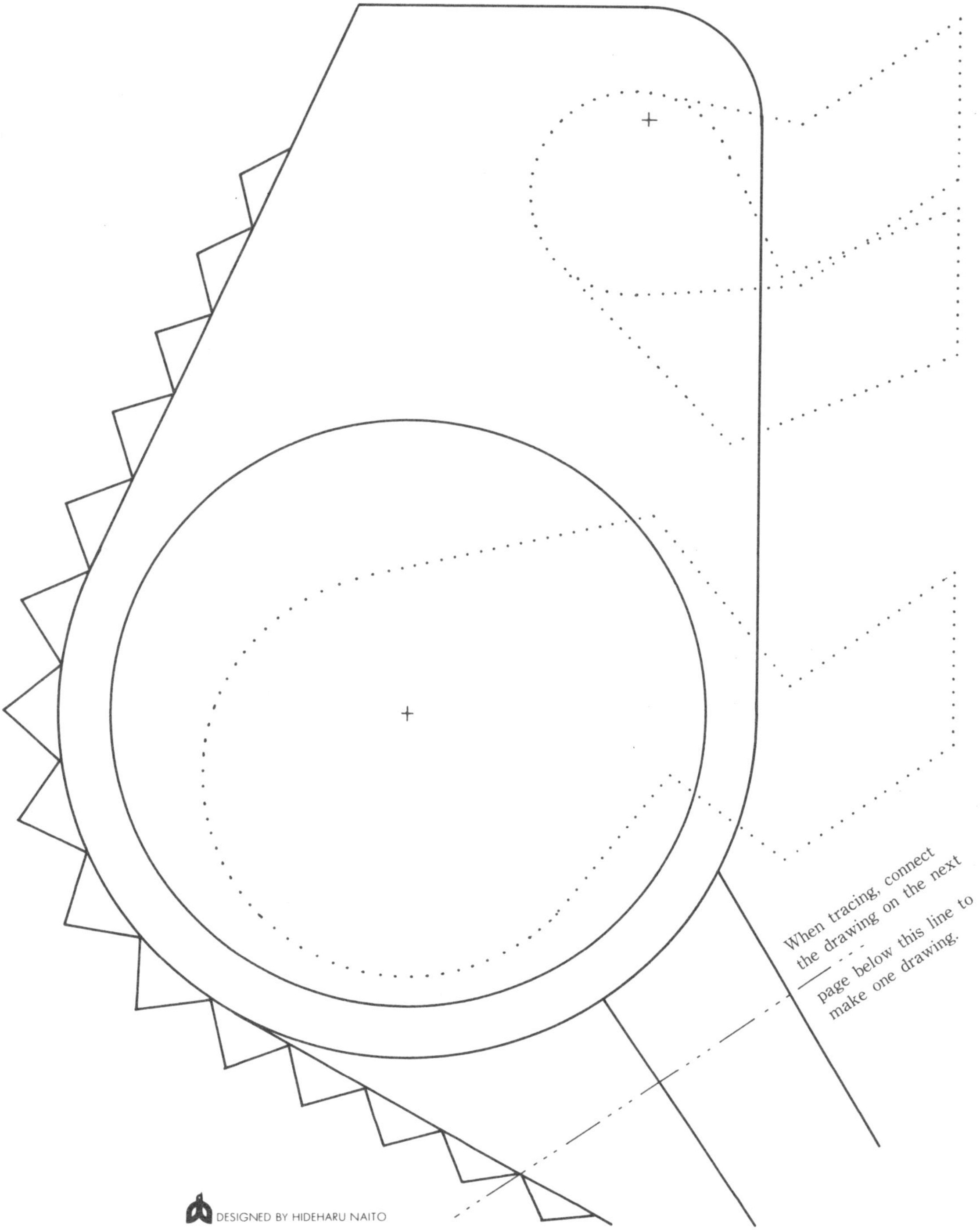

DESIGNED BY HIDEHARU NAITO

TRICERATOPS = ACTUAL-SIZE DRAWING〔III〕

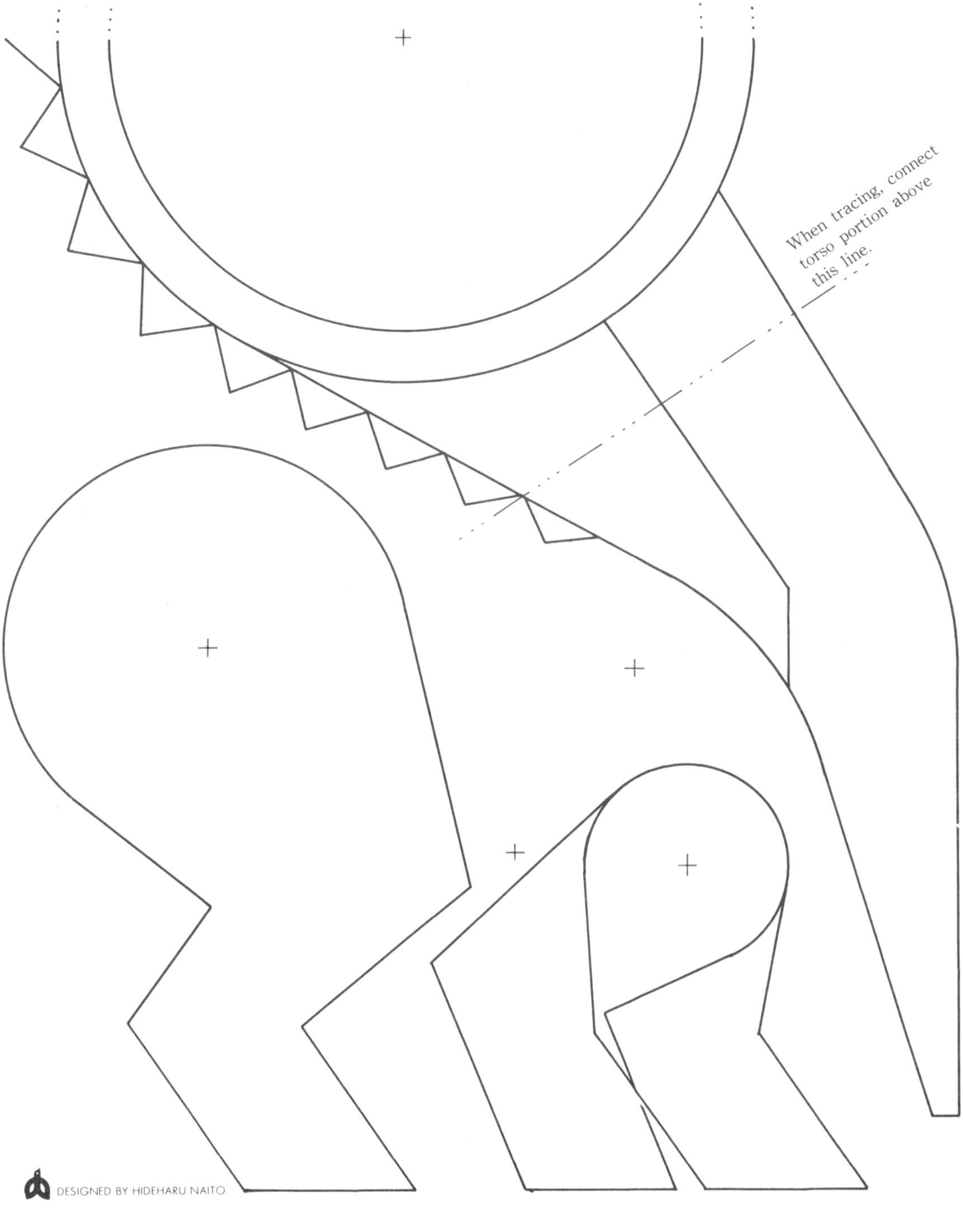

DESIGNED BY HIDEHARU NAITO

TRICERATOPS = ASSEMBLY INSTRUCTIONS

★ Double-check the number of parts

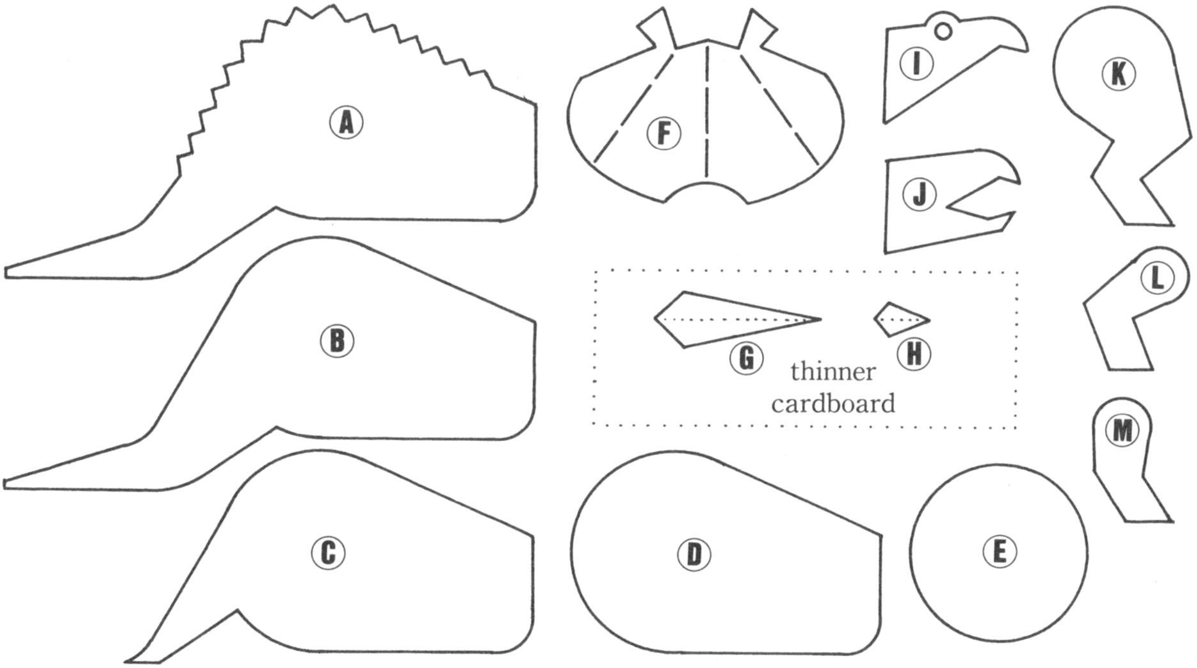

Ⓐ×1 Ⓑ×2 Ⓒ×2 Ⓓ×6 Ⓔ×2 Ⓕ×1 (slit the outer paper along the ——— mark to allow cardboard to bend) Ⓖ×2 (use outer paper of cardboard) Ⓗ×1 (cardboard outer paper) Ⓘ×2 Ⓙ×4 Ⓚ×6 Ⓛ×3 Ⓜ×3

1

After gluing the 4 Ⓙ head parts together, glue the Ⓘ parts on either side as shown.

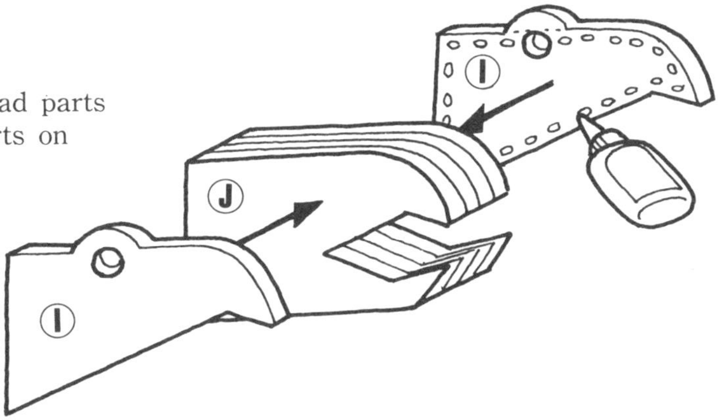

2

To build the torso, put the Ⓐ part in the middle, and glue on both sides of it, in turn, the Ⓑ, Ⓒ, Ⓓ, and Ⓔ parts. Use a triangle to make the parts stand vertically and to give the torso a good shape.

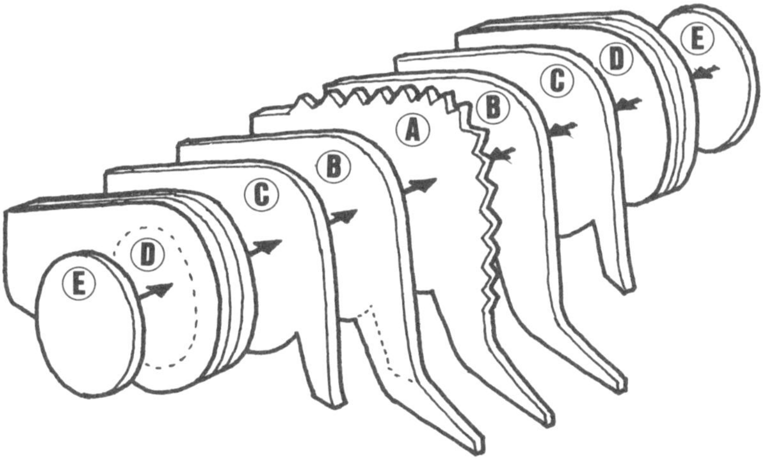

3

Use the actual-size drawing to trace the location of the legs onto the torso. Make the legs Ⓚ, Ⓛ, Ⓜ, and attach them to the torso. Glue on the head as shown. Fold the Ⓕ, Ⓖ and Ⓗ parts and glue on.

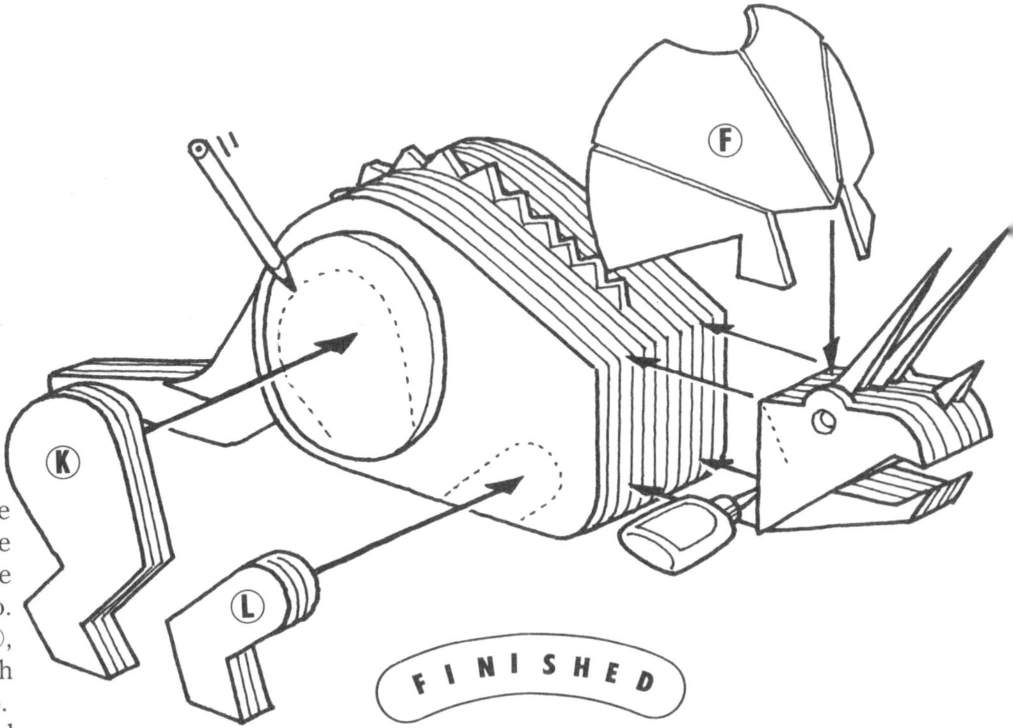

FINISHED

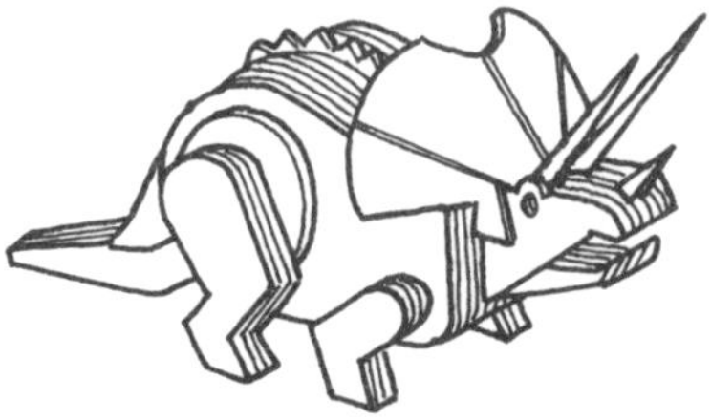

STYRACOSAURUS

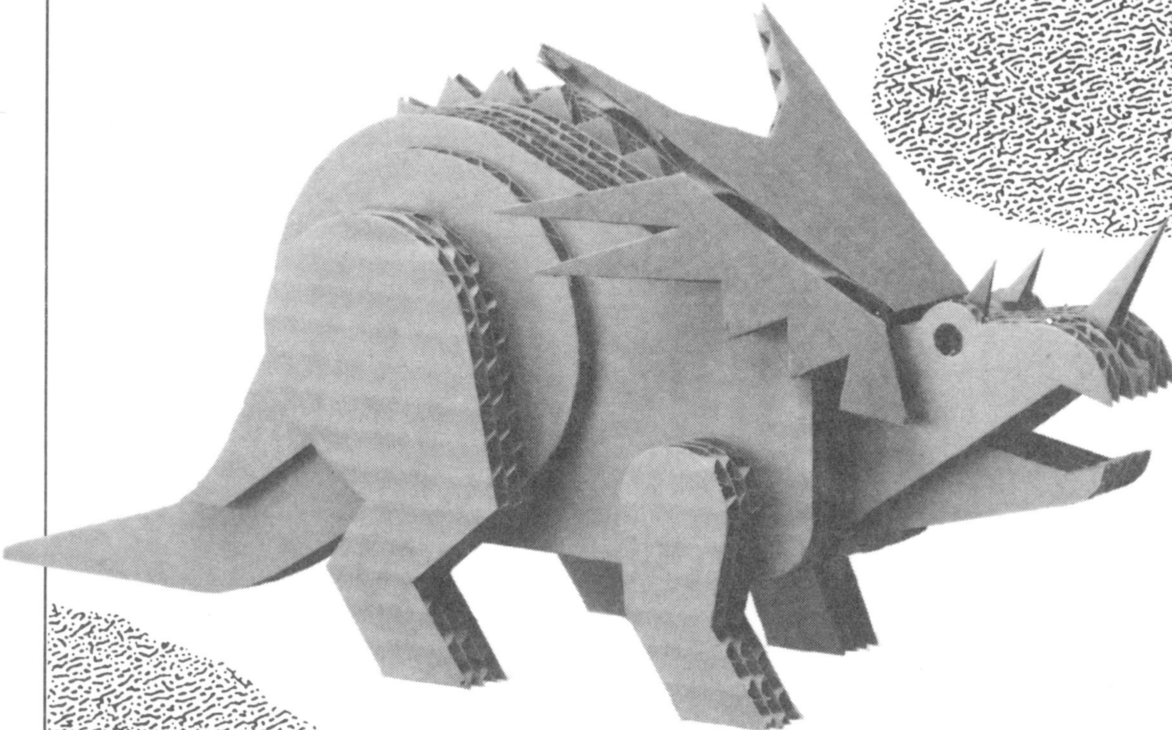

side view

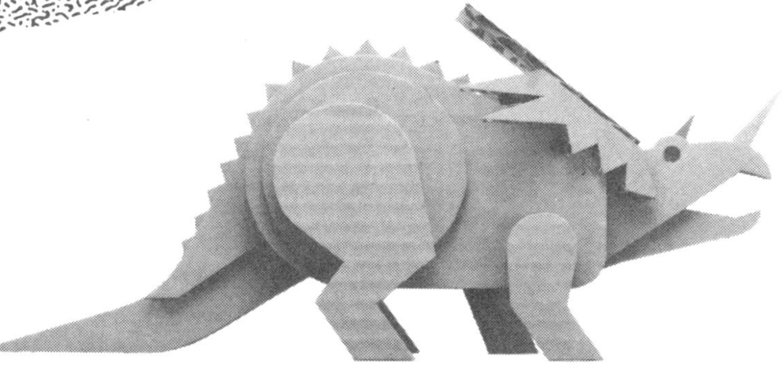

front view

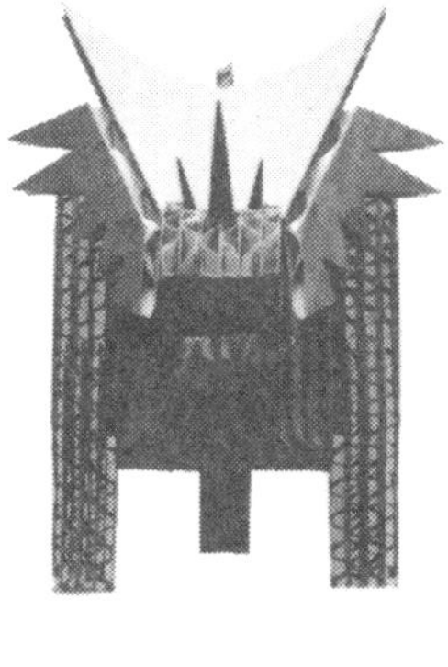

STYRACOSAURUS = ACTUAL-SIZE DRAWING

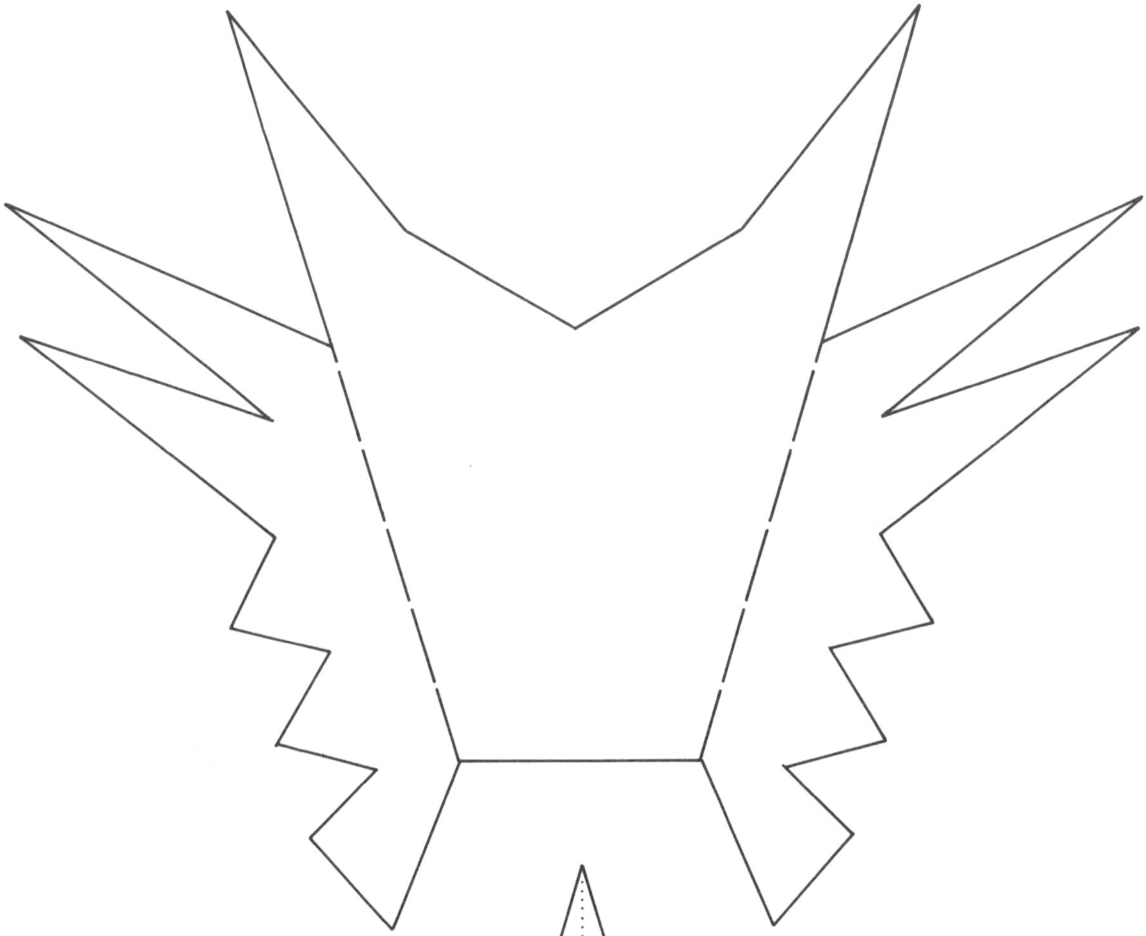

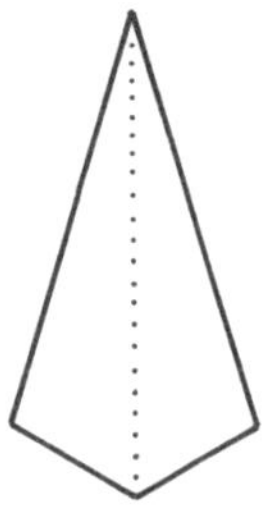

※Except for the collar and the top of the head, this dinosaur is the same as the Triceratops.

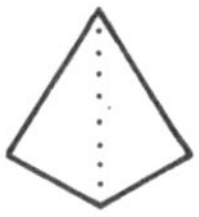

★ Double-check the number of parts

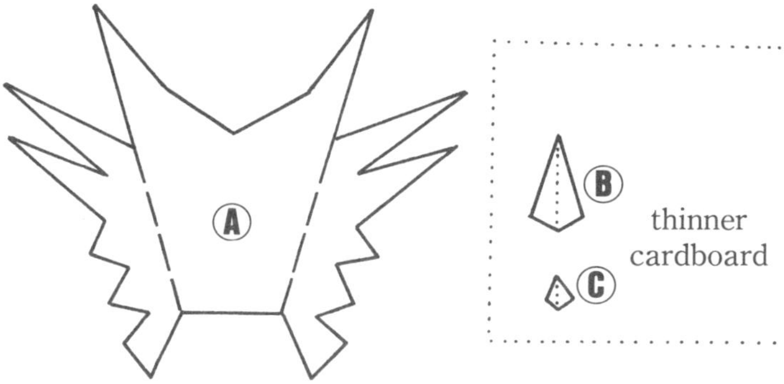

Ⓐ × 1 (slit outer paper along the — — marks to help fold cardboard)
Ⓑ × 1 (cardboard outer paper) Ⓒ × 2 (cardboard outer paper)

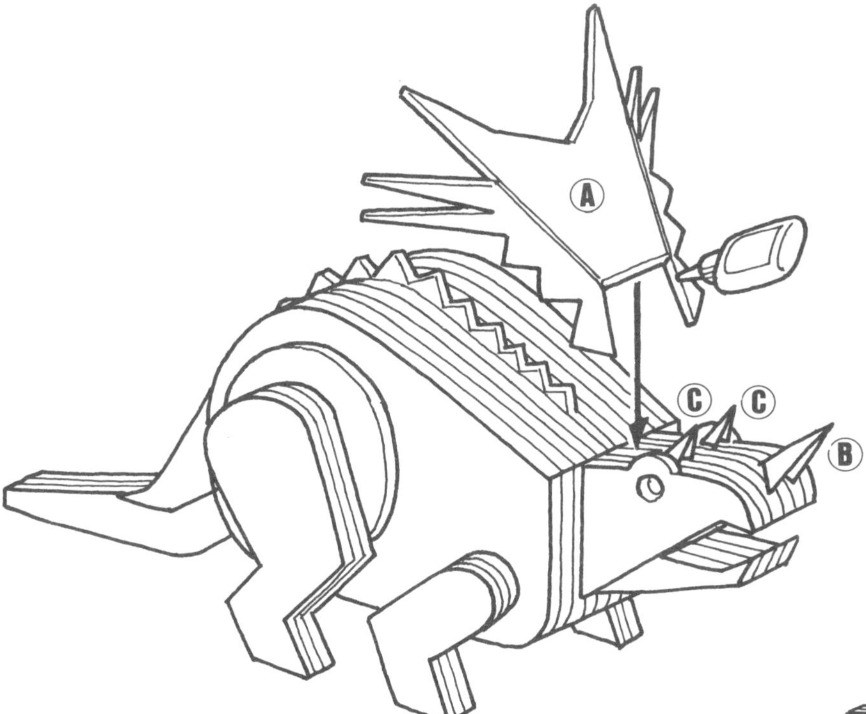

1

Build the torso the same way as for the Triceratops. Cut lightly along the — — folding lines of the collar Ⓐ, fold, and glue on. Then, as shown, fold and glue on parts Ⓑ and Ⓒ.

FINISHED

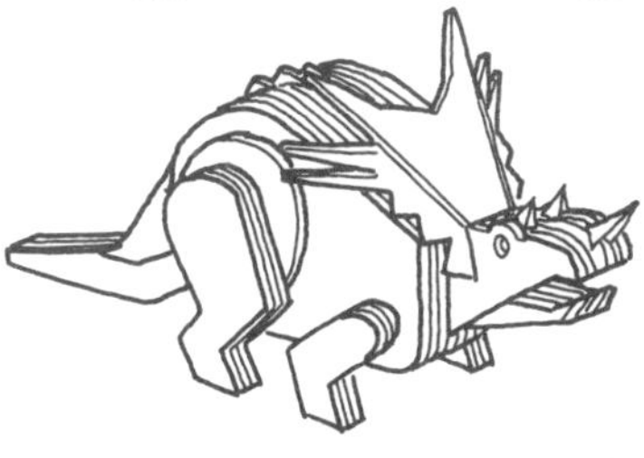

STEGOSAURUS

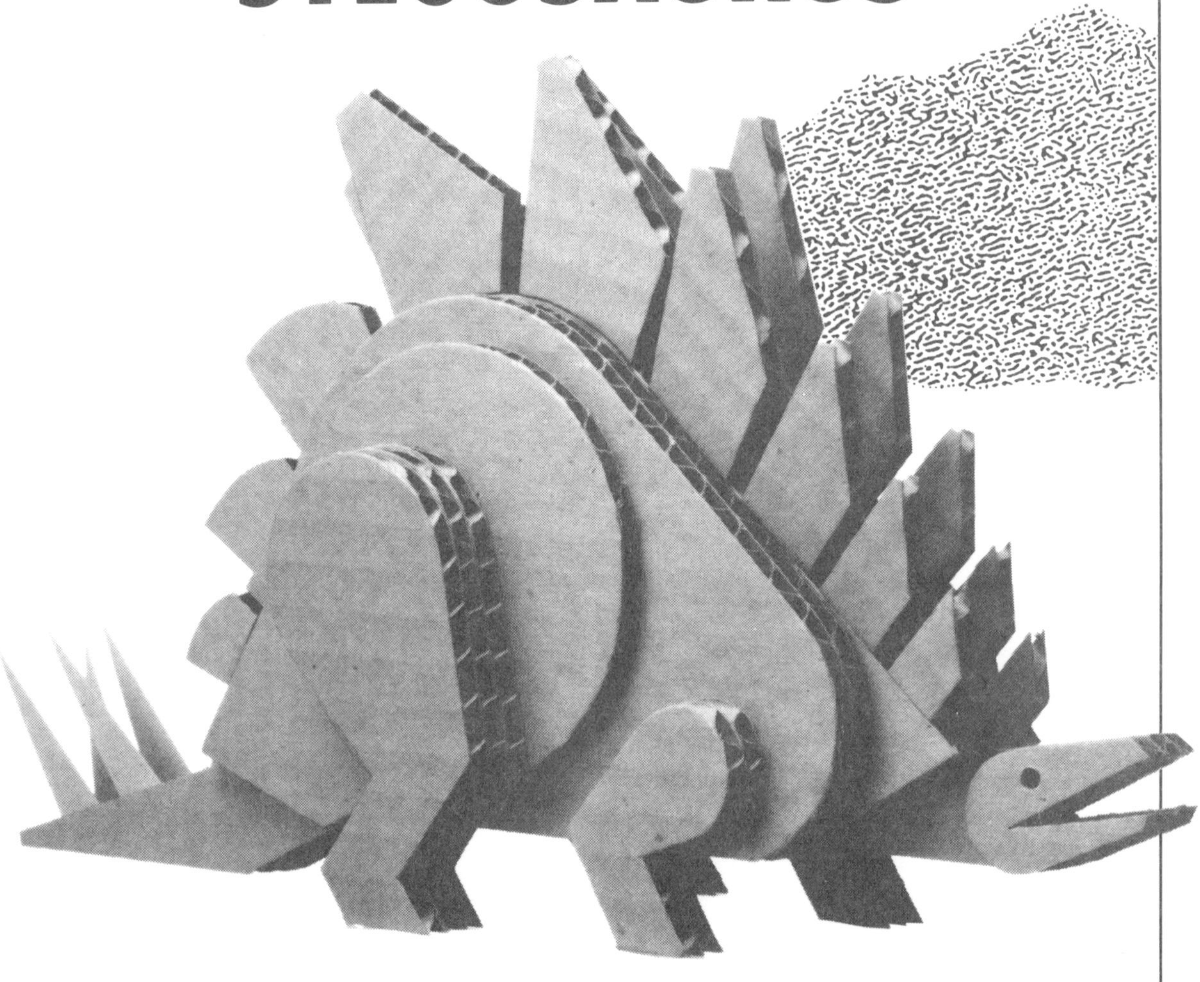

side view

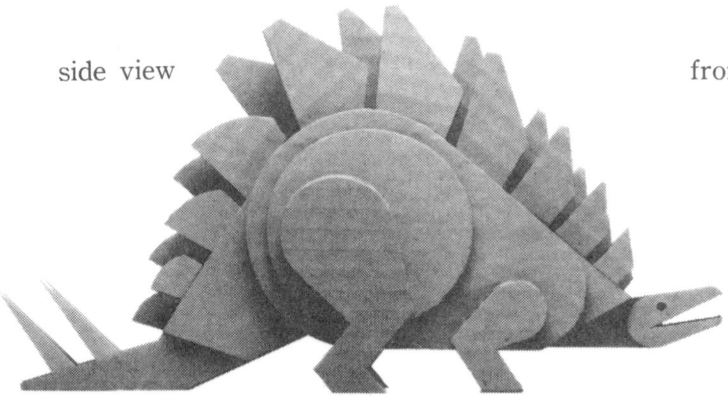

front view

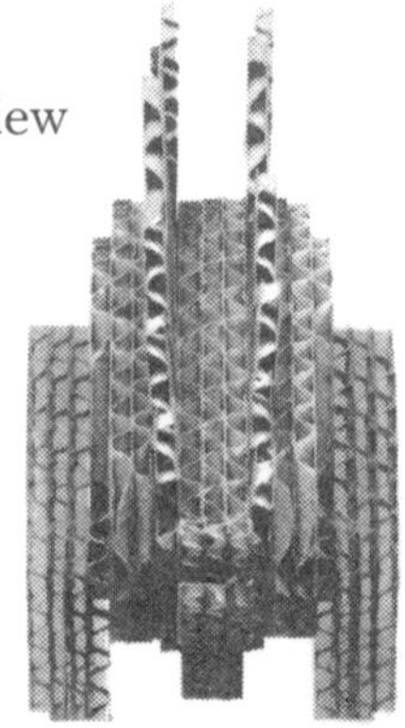

STEGOSAURUS = ACTUAL-SIZE DRAWING〔 I 〕

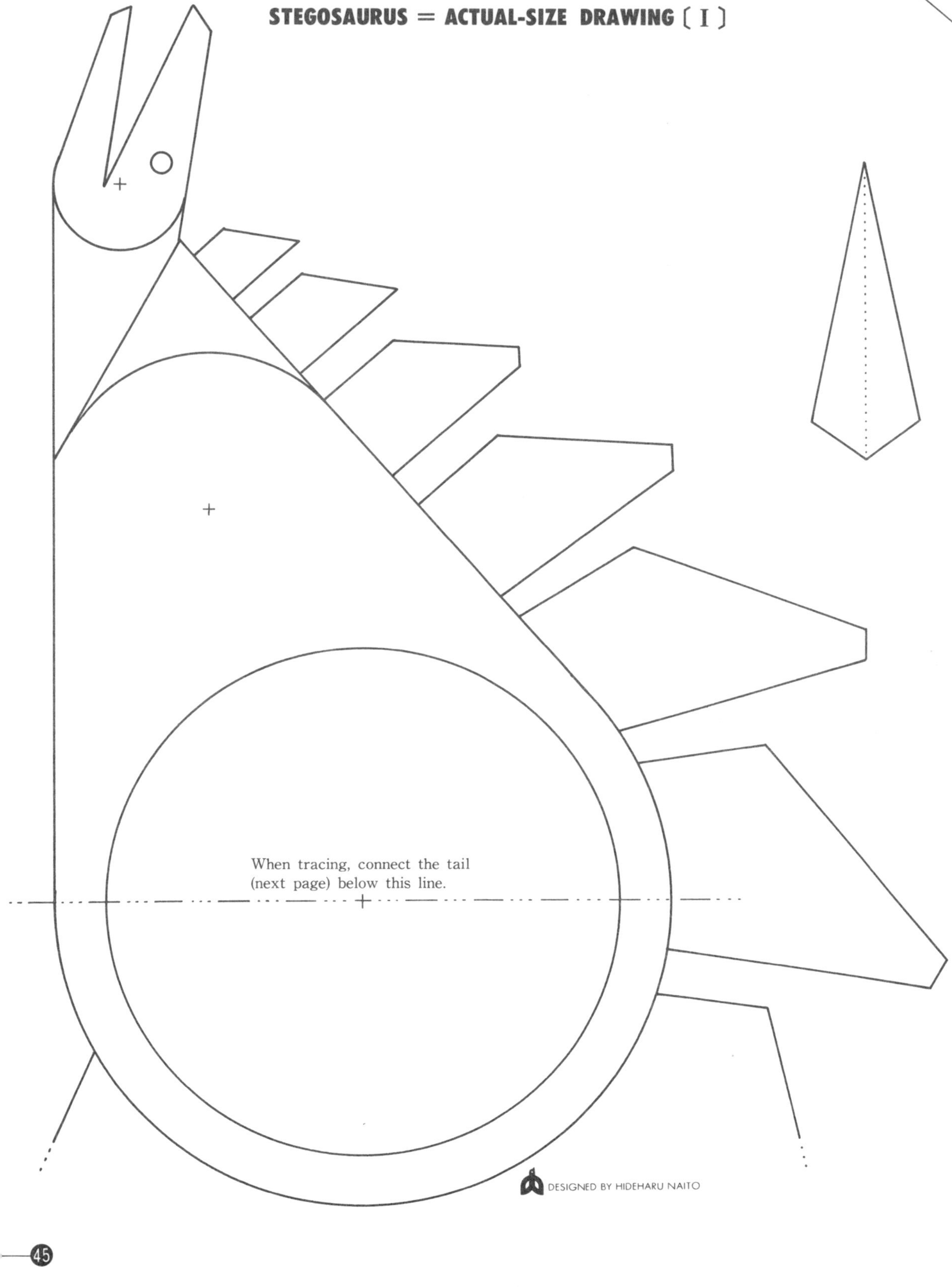

DESIGNED BY HIDEHARU NAITO

STEGOSAURUS = ACTUAL-SIZE DRAWING 〔II〕

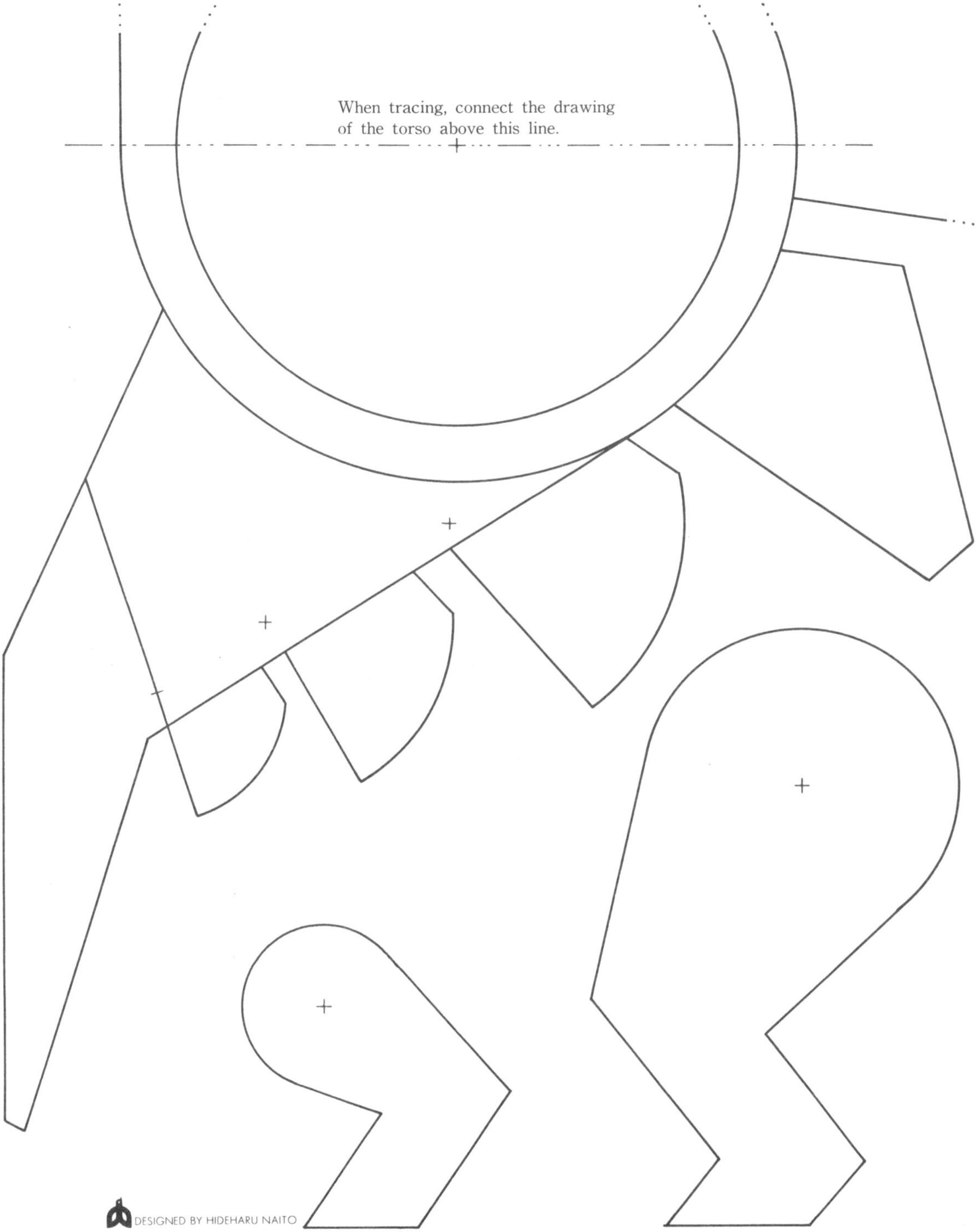

DESIGNED BY HIDEHARU NAITO

STEGOSAURUS = ASSEMBLY INSTRUCTIONS

★ Double-check the number of parts

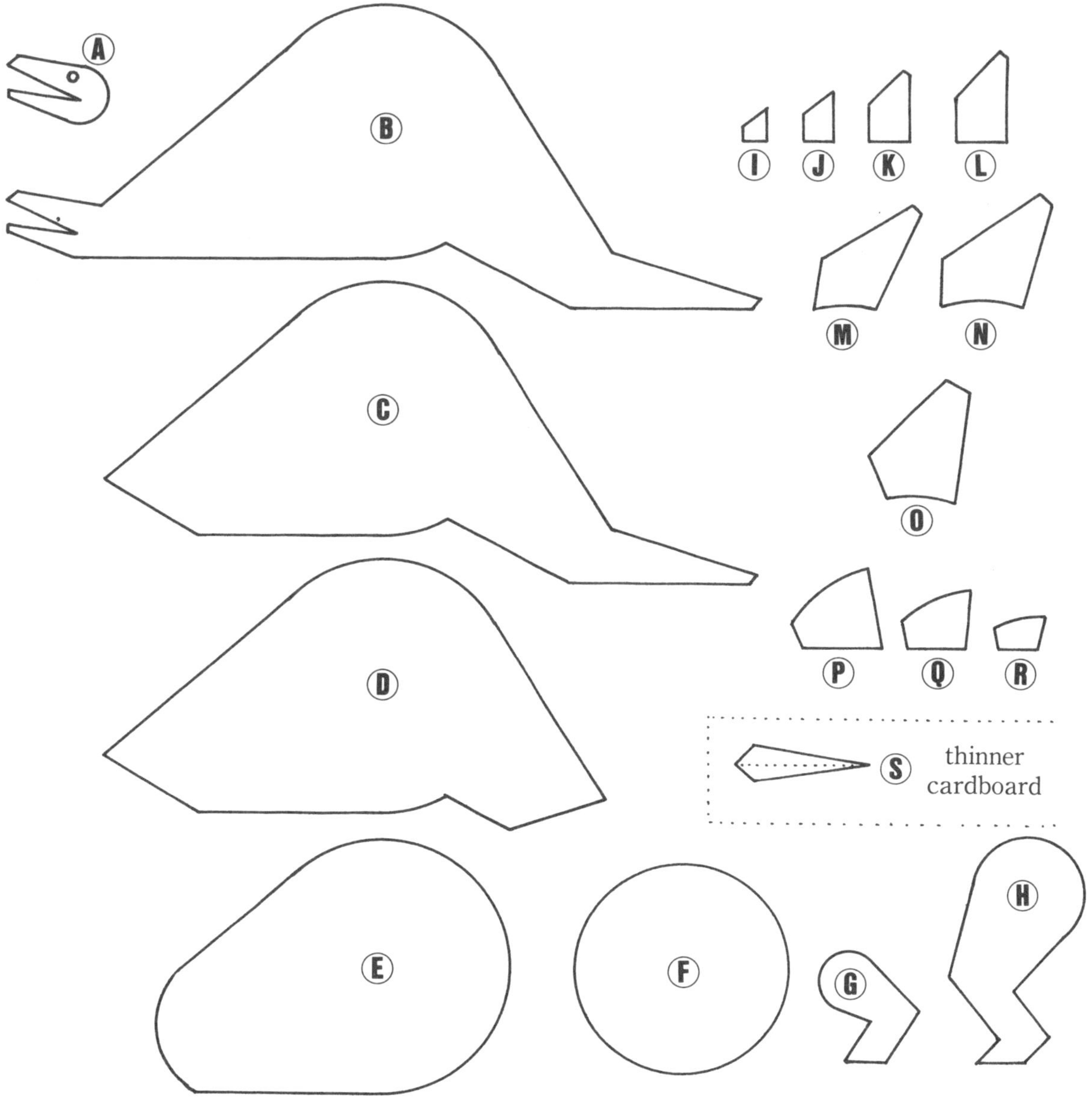

Ⓐ×2 Ⓑ×1 Ⓒ×2 Ⓓ×2 Ⓔ×4 Ⓕ×2 Ⓖ×4 Ⓗ×6 Ⓘ×1
Ⓙ to Ⓡ×2 each Ⓢ×4 (thinner cardboard)

1

To build the torso, put the Ⓑ part in the middle, and glue on both sides of it, in turn, the Ⓒ,Ⓓ,Ⓔ (2 on each side) and Ⓕ parts, as shown.

Dab the glue on at $\frac{1}{4}''$ to $\frac{1}{2}''$ (5mm to 10mm) intervals.

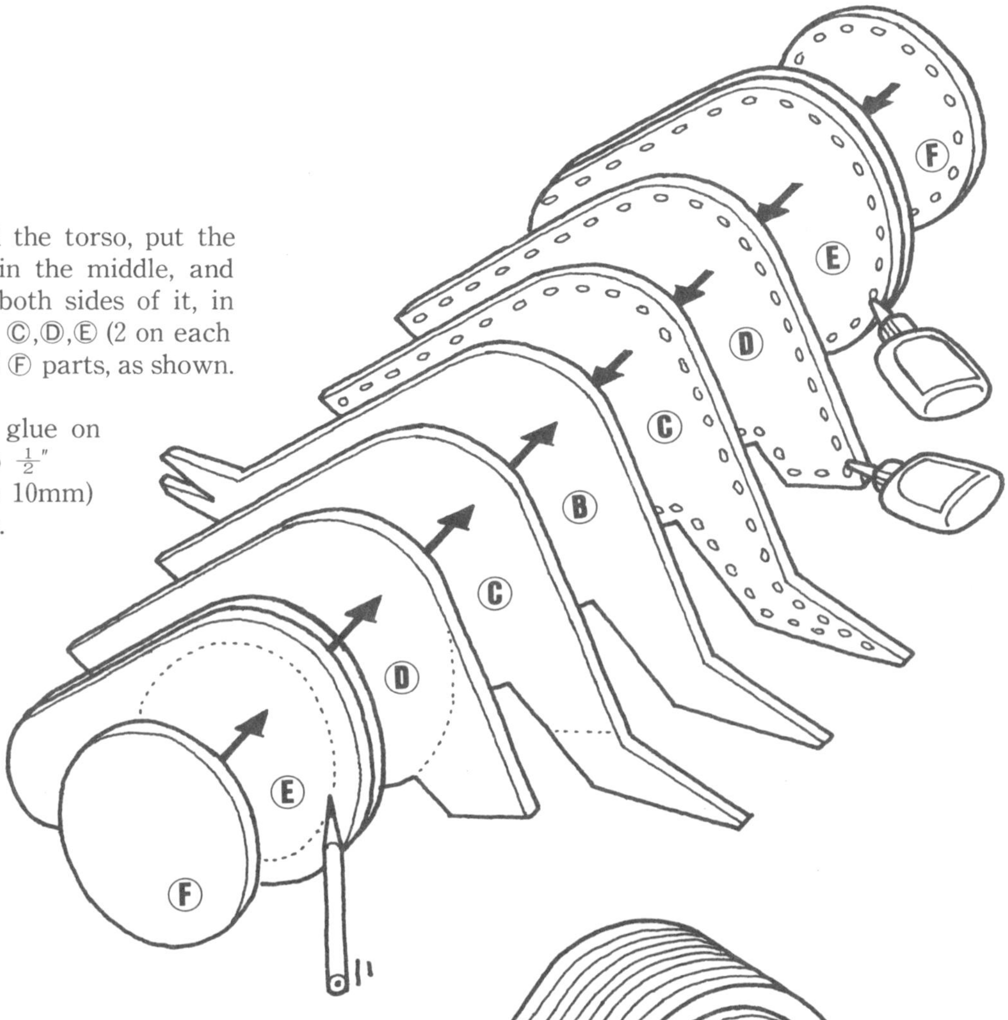

2

Following the diagram, attach the 2 parts of the head Ⓐ to the finished torso.

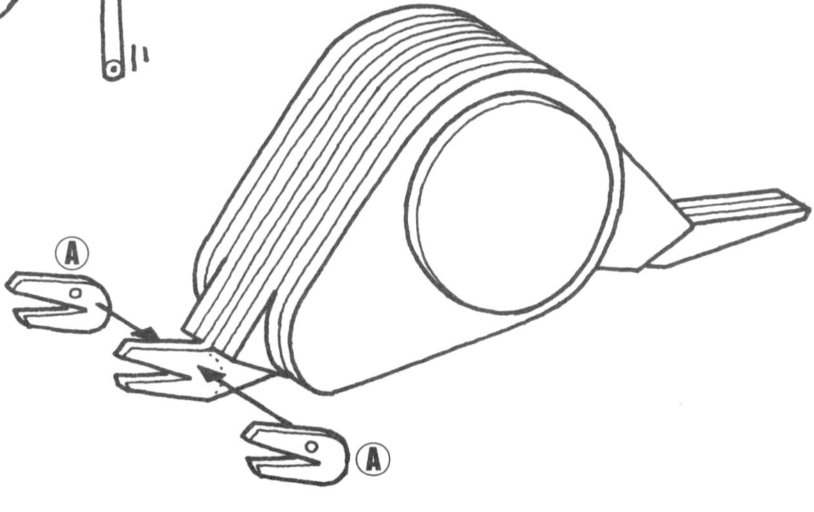

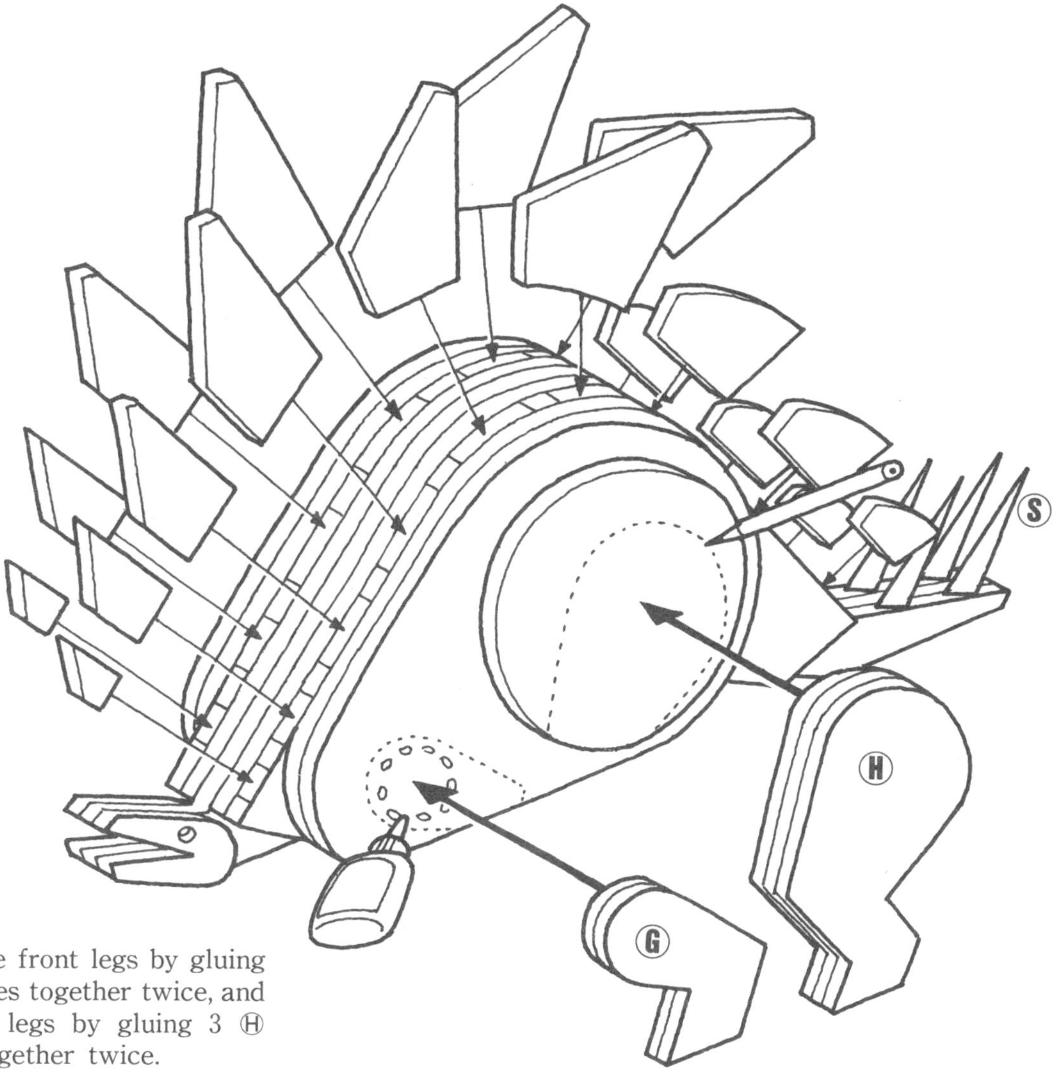

3

Make the front legs by gluing 2 Ⓖ pieces together twice, and the rear legs by gluing 3 Ⓗ pieces together twice.
Use the actual-size drawing to trace the location of the legs onto the torso.
Fold the spikes Ⓢ (made of the outer layer of the cardboard) and glue on as shown.
As shown in the diagram, glue on parts Ⓘ through Ⓡ. (See photograph, too)

FINISHED

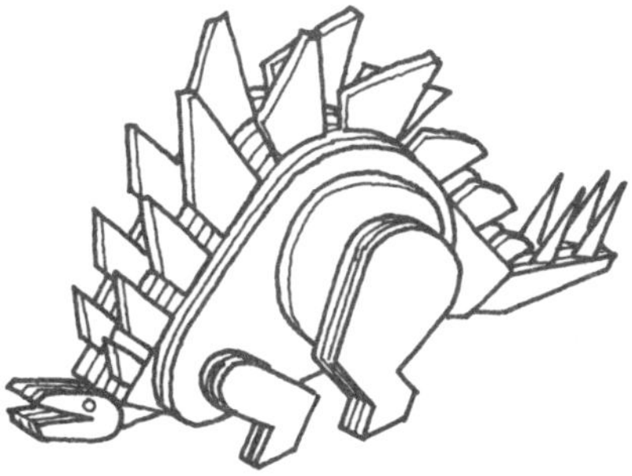

DIMETRODON (Pencil Holder)

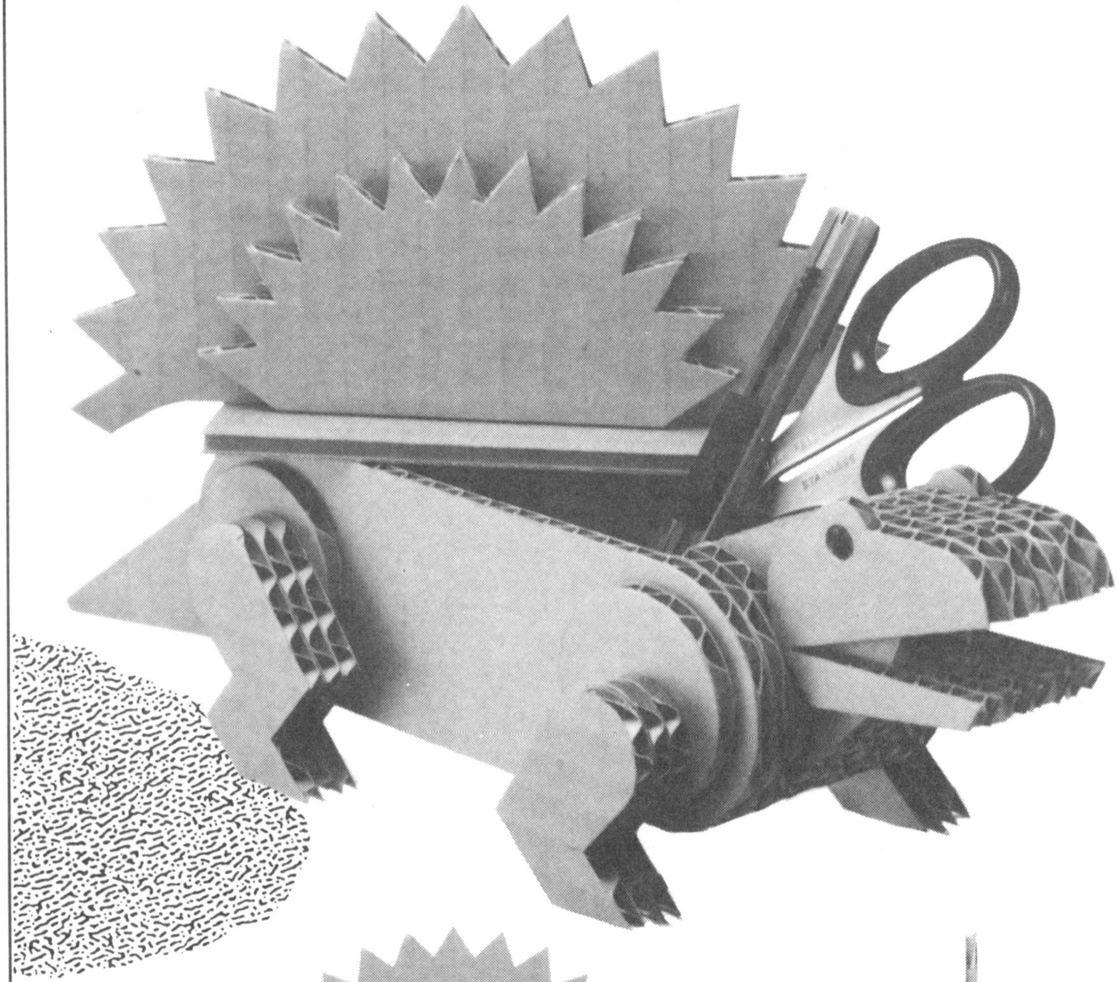

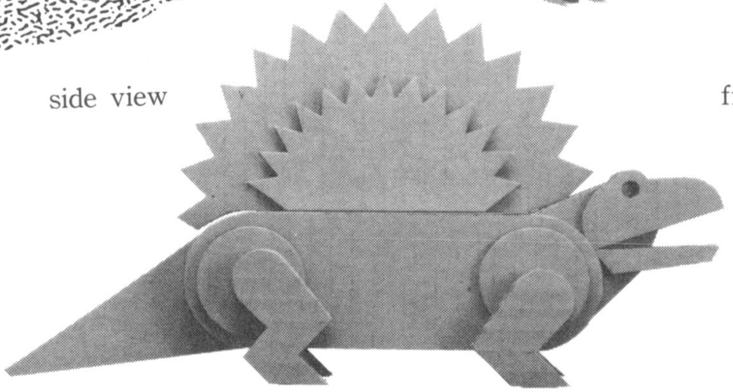

side view

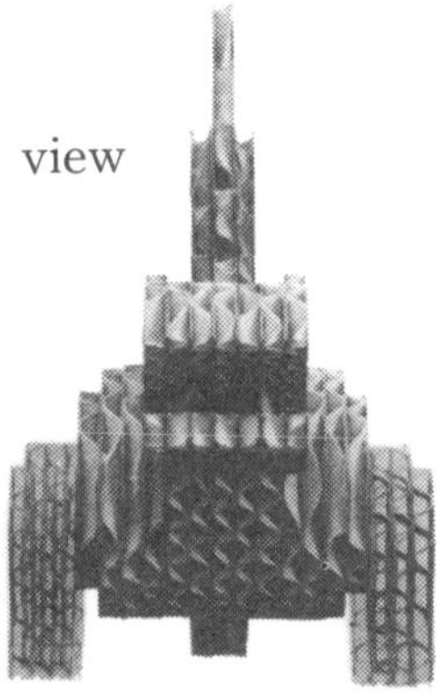

front view

DIMETRODON = ACTUAL-SIZE DRAWING〔I〕

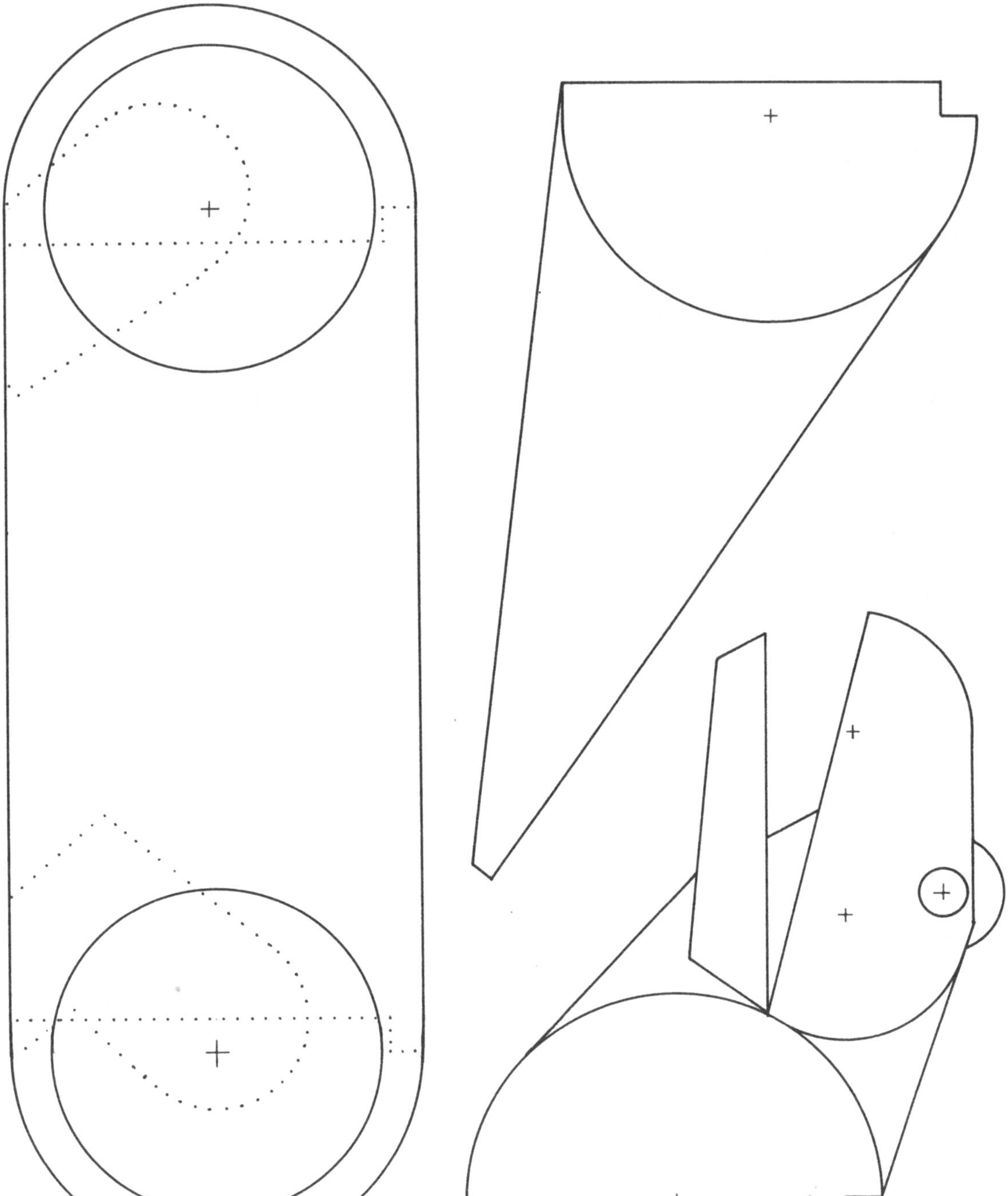

DESIGNED BY HIDEHARU NAITO

DIMETRODON ACTUAL-SIZE DRAWING〔II〕

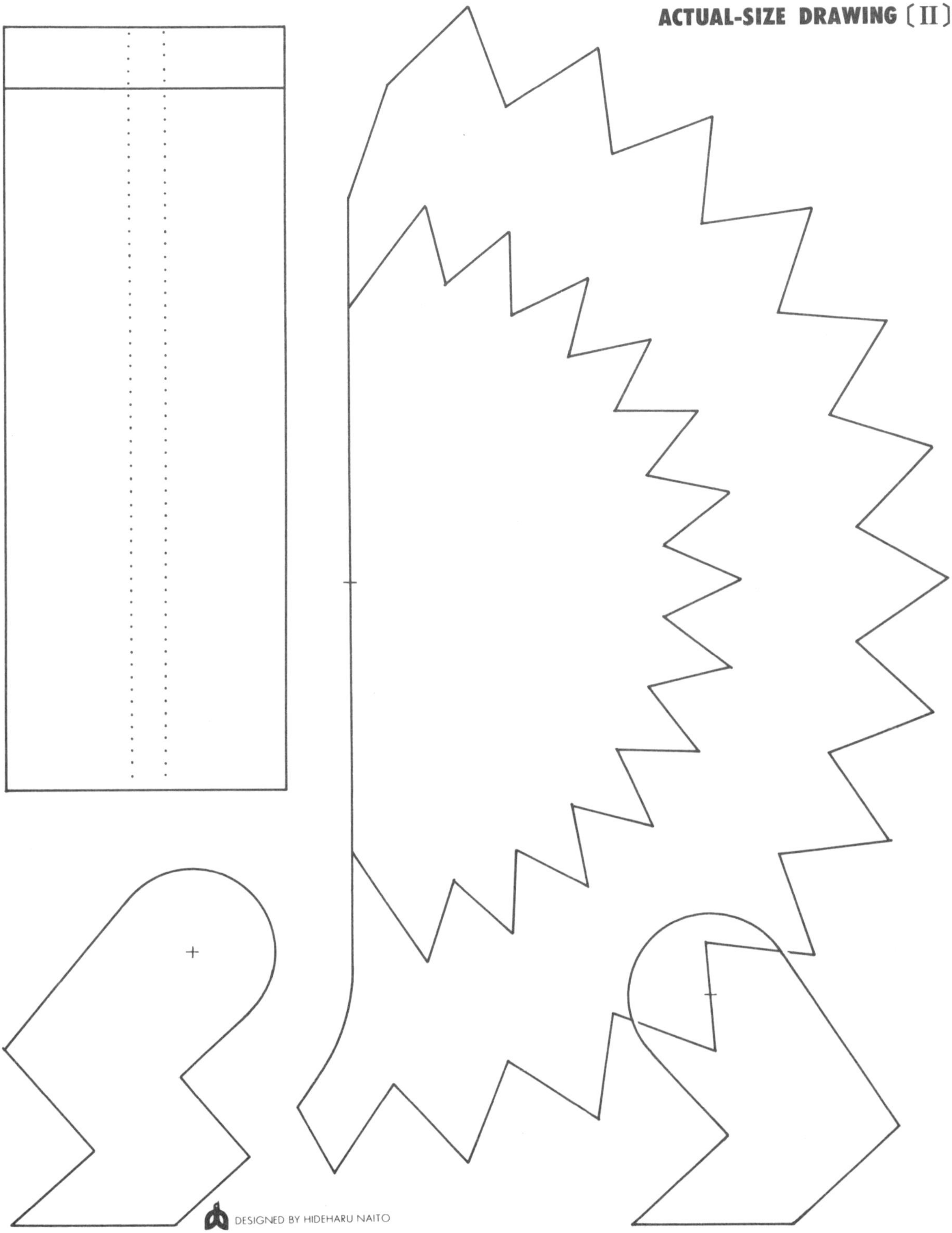

DESIGNED BY HIDEHARU NAITO

DIMETRODON = ASSEMBLY INSTRUCTIONS

★ Double-check the number of parts

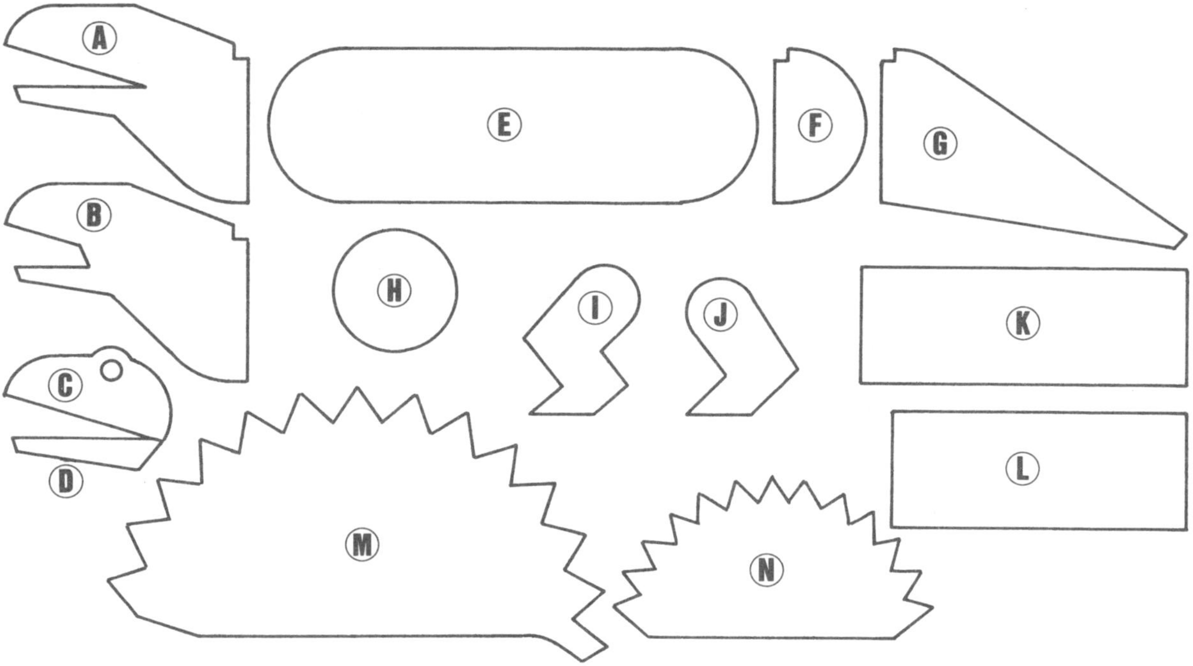

Ⓐ×3 Ⓑ×2 Ⓒ×2 Ⓓ×2 Ⓔ×2 Ⓕ×10 Ⓖ×3
Ⓗ×4 Ⓘ×6 Ⓙ×6 Ⓚ×1 Ⓛ×1 Ⓜ×1 Ⓝ×2

1 To make the back, put the Ⓜ part in the middle, and glue the Ⓝ parts on either side. Use a triangle to keep the parts vertical. Glue the back to the Ⓚ part.

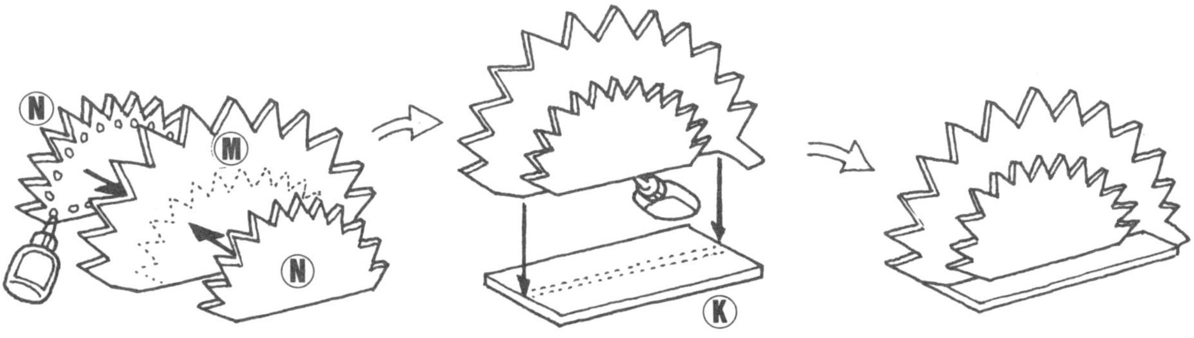

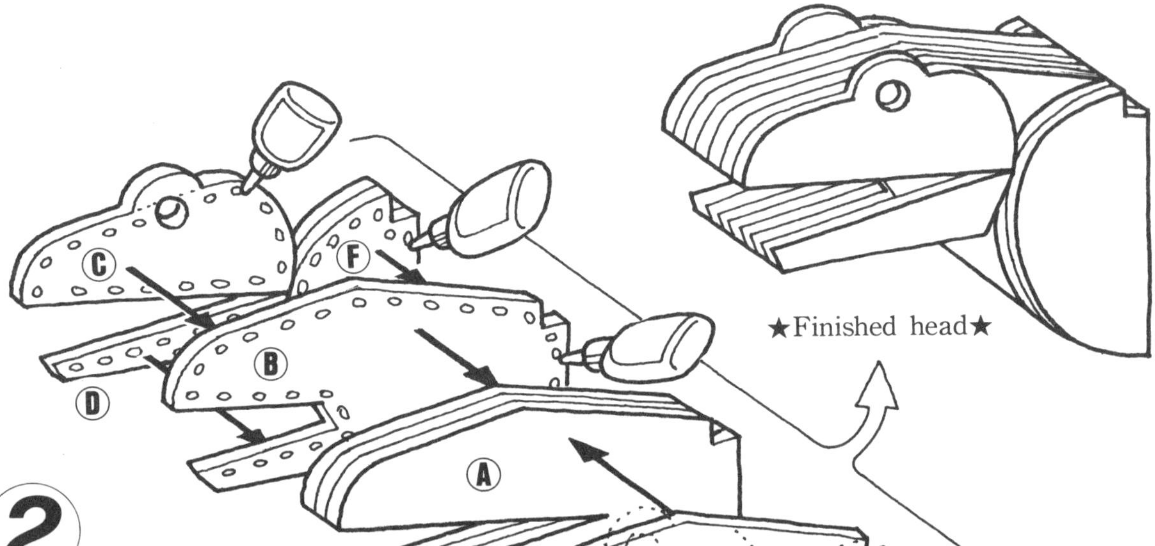

2

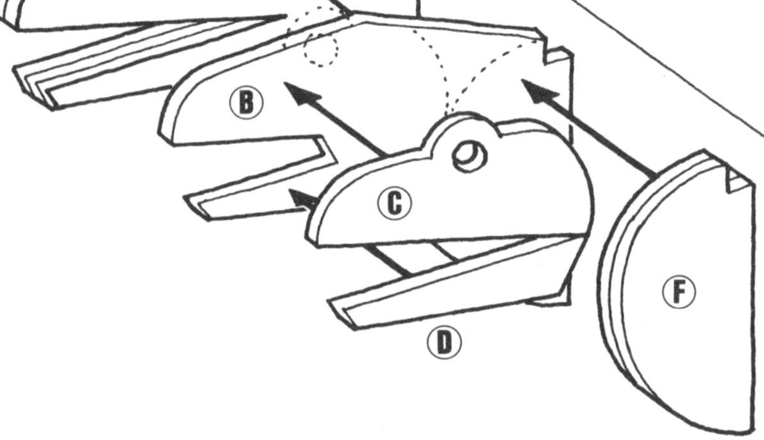

To make the head, glue the 3 middle Ⓐ parts together. On either side of that, in turn, glue on the Ⓑ, Ⓒ and Ⓓ parts. Next, glue 2 Ⓕ parts on each side, as shown. Dab the glue at $\frac{1}{4}$" to $\frac{1}{2}$" (5mm to 10mm) intervals.

3

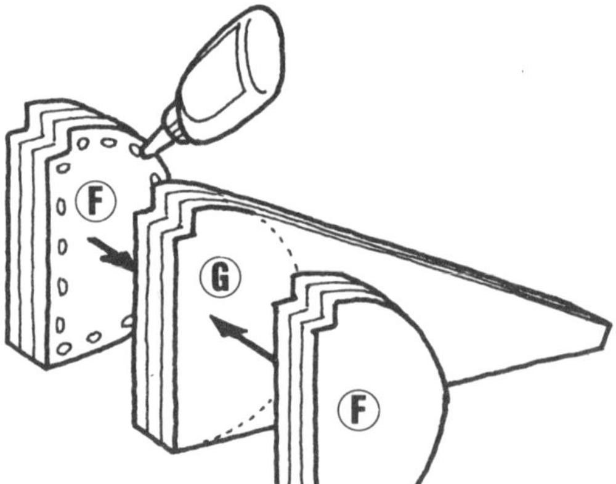

To build the tail, first glue the 3 Ⓖ parts together. Glue the Ⓕ parts together in 2 groups of 3 and glue onto either side of the Ⓖ parts.

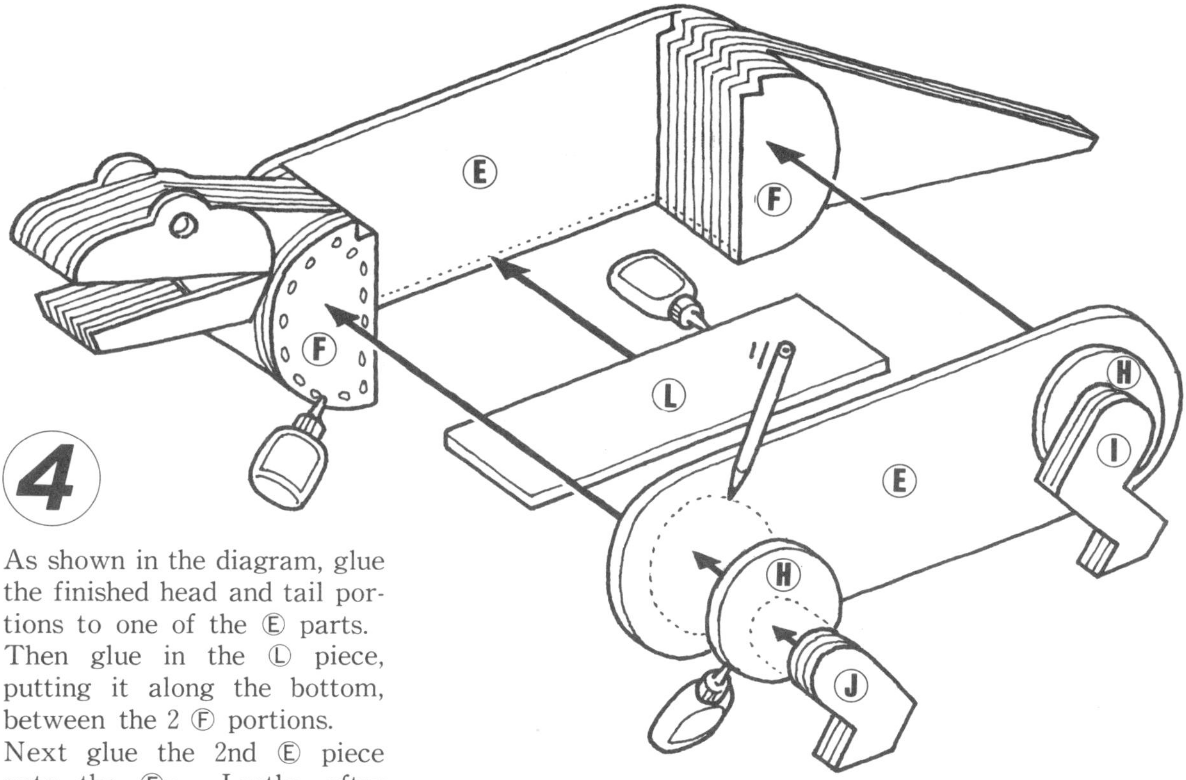

4

As shown in the diagram, glue the finished head and tail portions to one of the Ⓔ parts. Then glue in the Ⓛ piece, putting it along the bottom, between the 2 Ⓕ portions. Next glue the 2nd Ⓔ piece onto the Ⓕs. Lastly, after using the actual-size drawing to trace on the location of the legs, assemble and attach the legs Ⓗ, Ⓘ and Ⓙ.

FINISHED

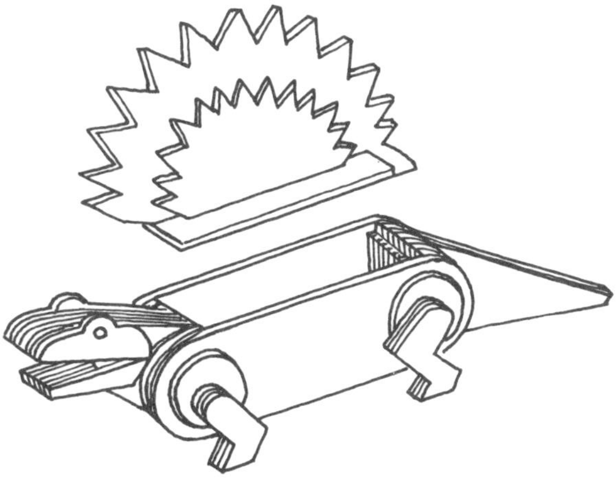

TYRANNOSAURUS

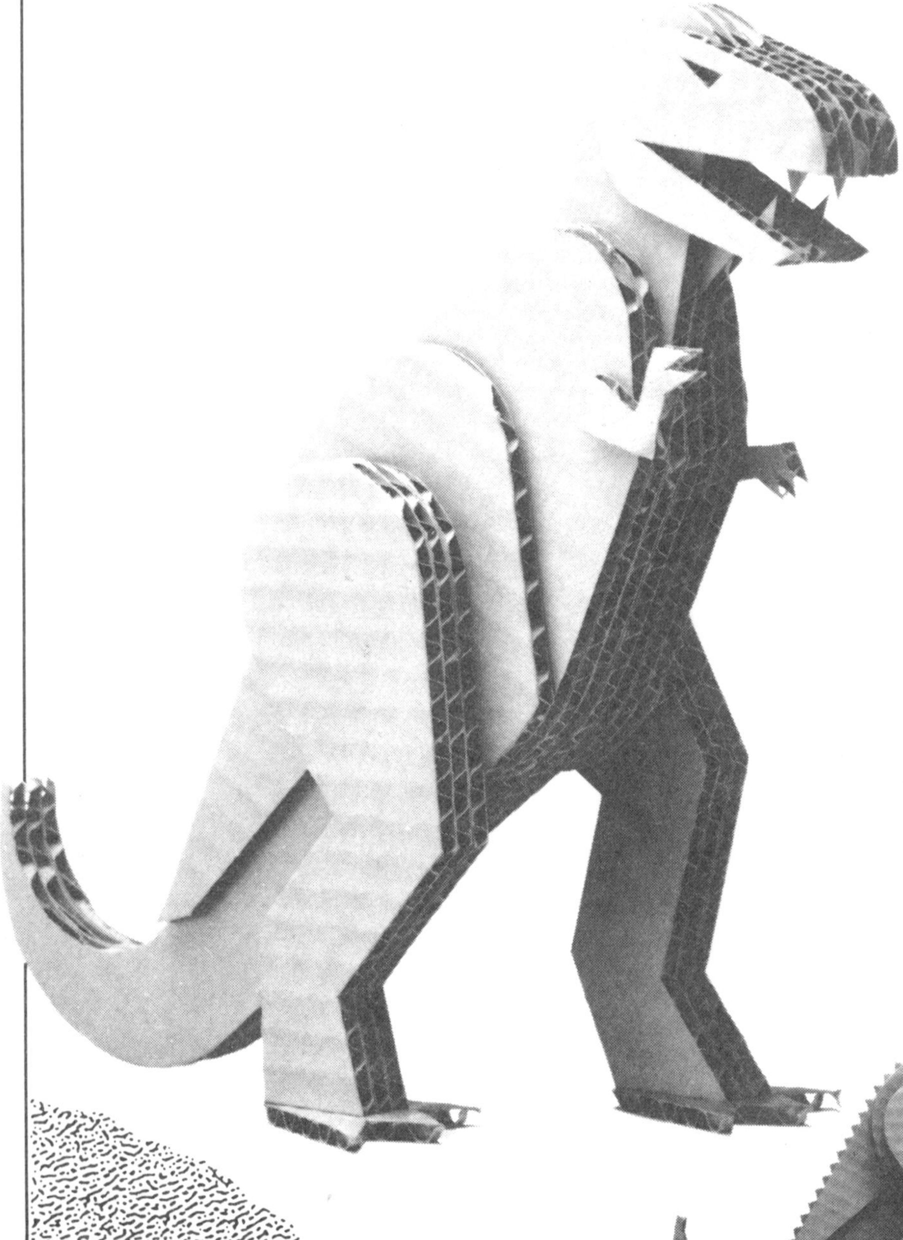

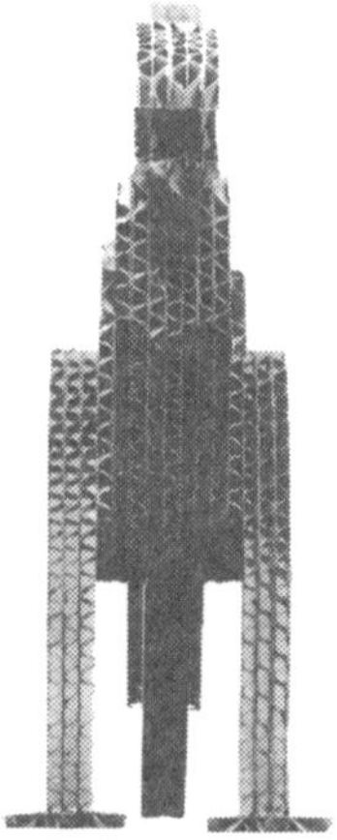

front view

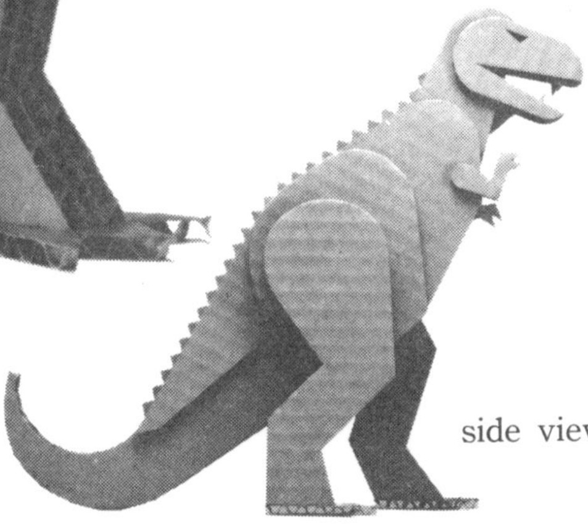

side view

TYRANNOSAURUS = ACTUAL-SIZE DRAWING〔I〕

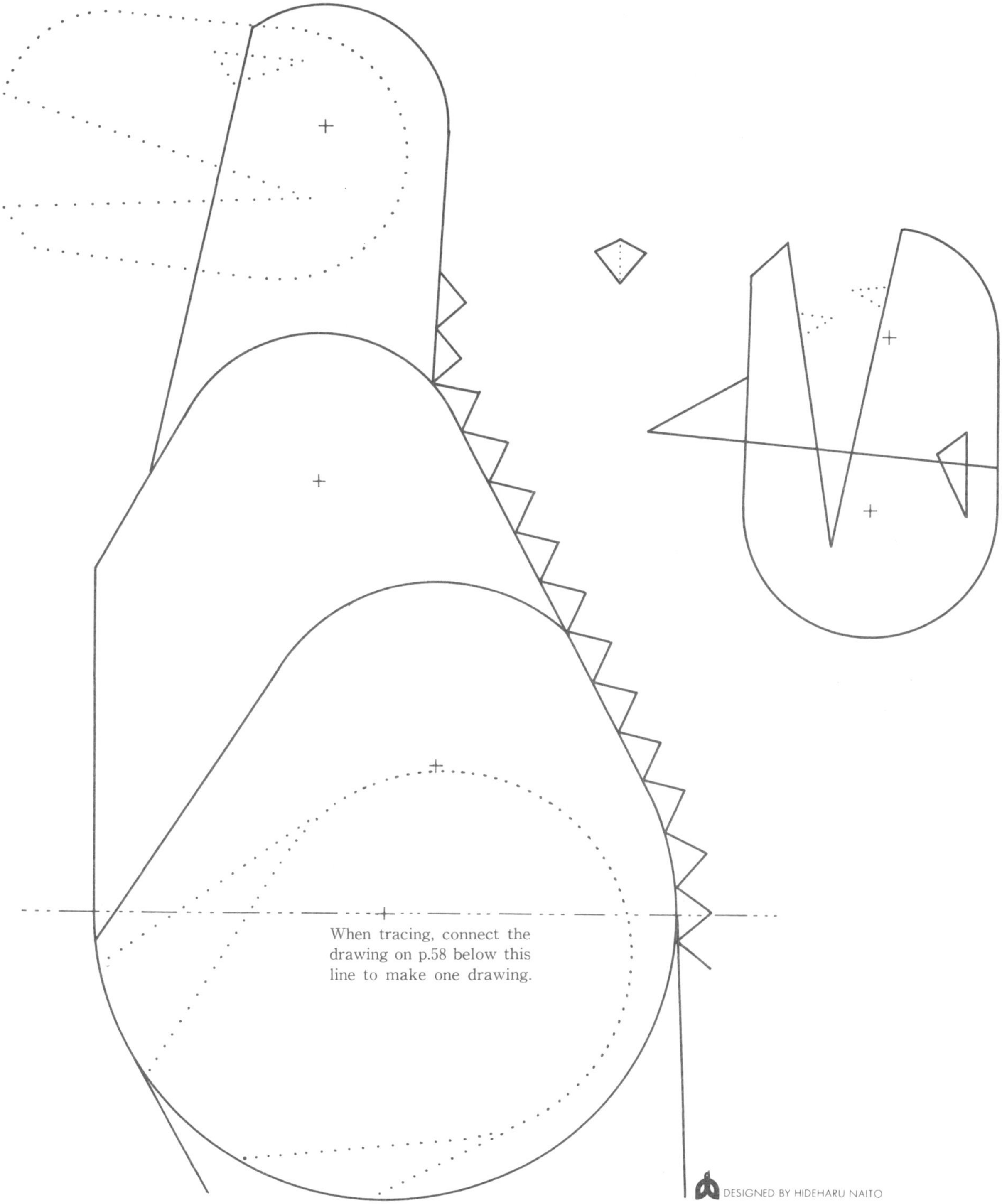

DESIGNED BY HIDEHARU NAITO

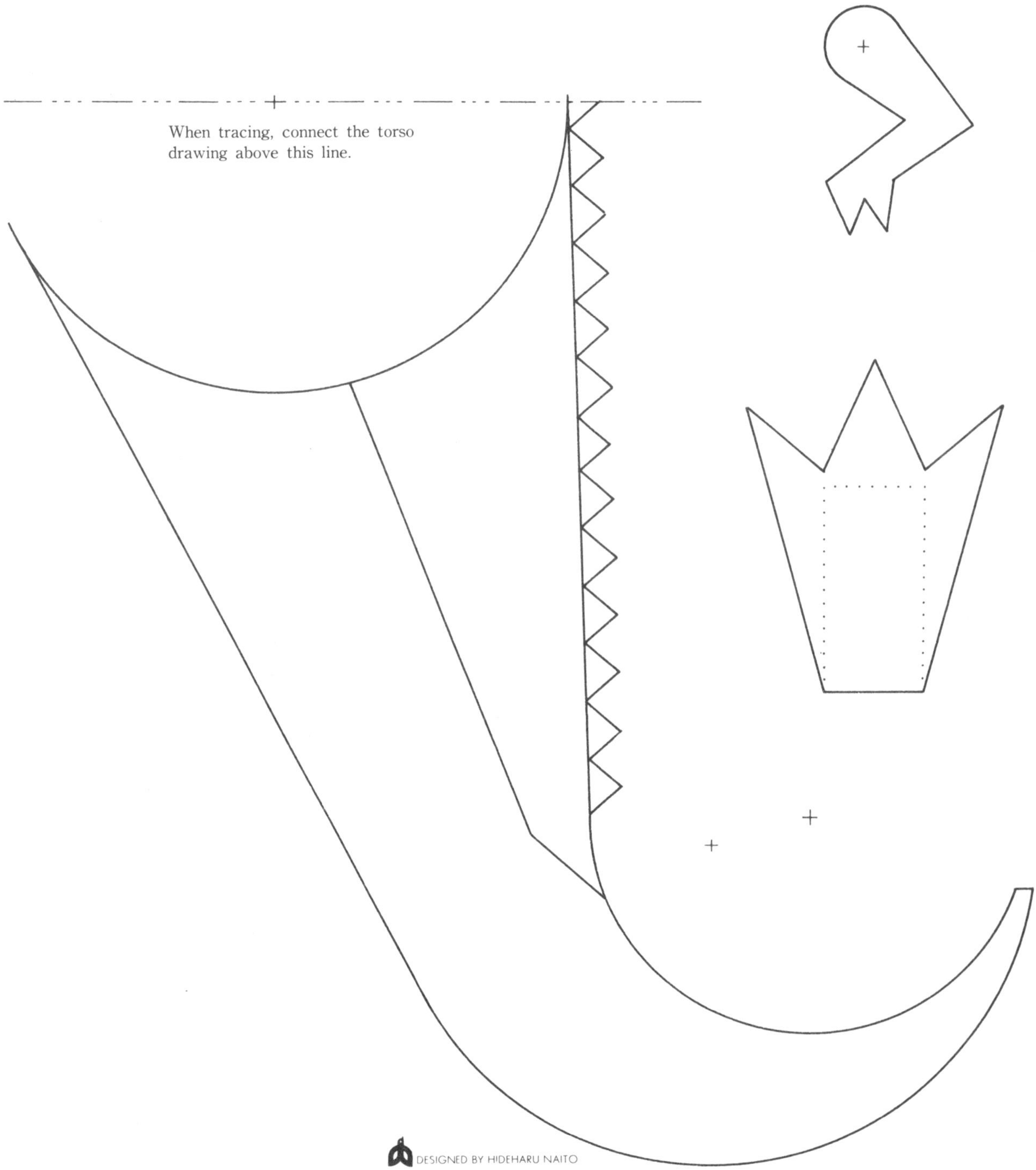

DESIGNED BY HIDEHARU NAITO

TYRANNOSAURUS = ACTUAL-SIZE DRAWING (III)

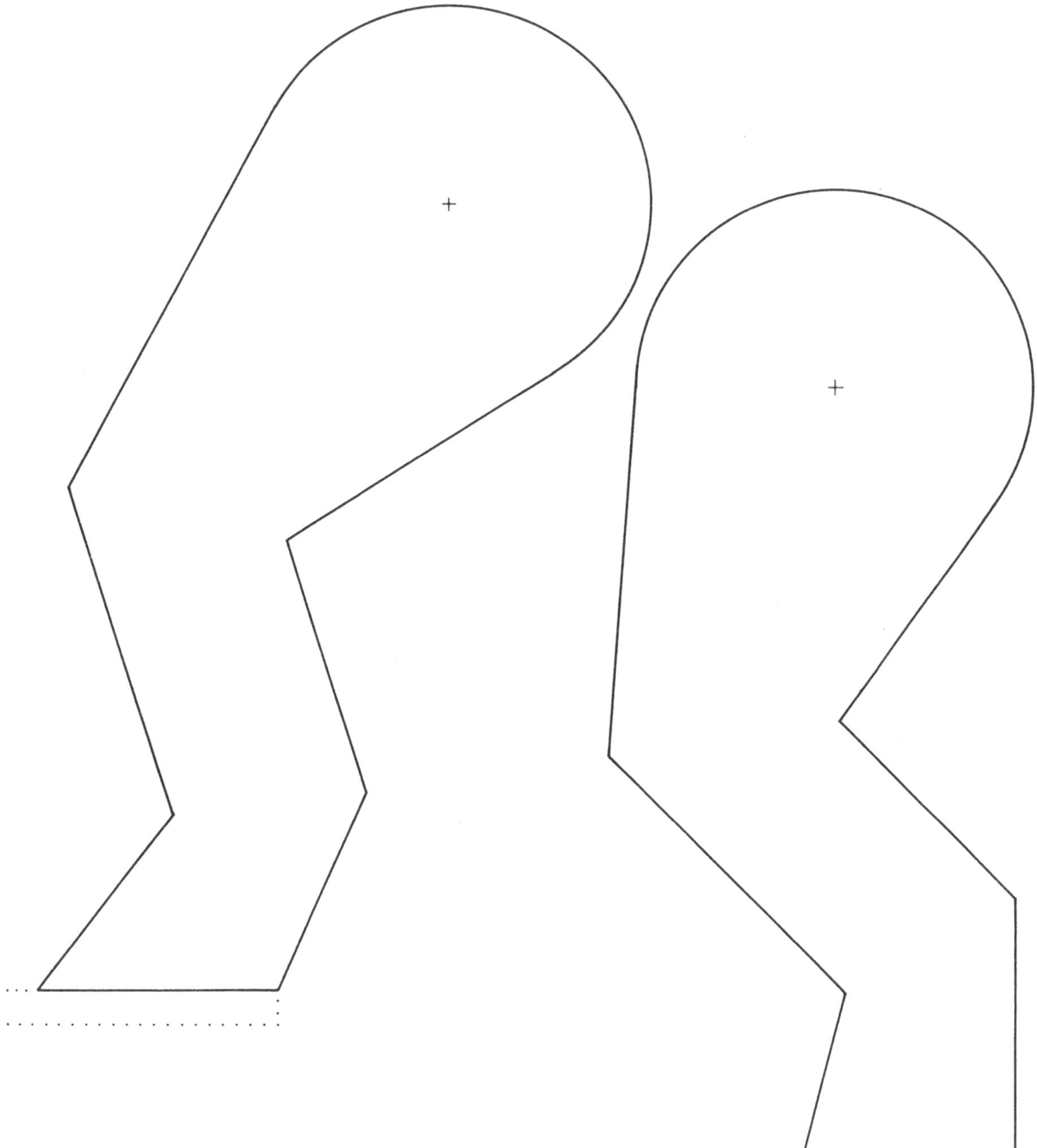

DESIGNED BY HIDEHARU NAITO

TYRANNOSAURUS = ASSEMBLY INSTRUCTIONS

★ Double-check the number of parts

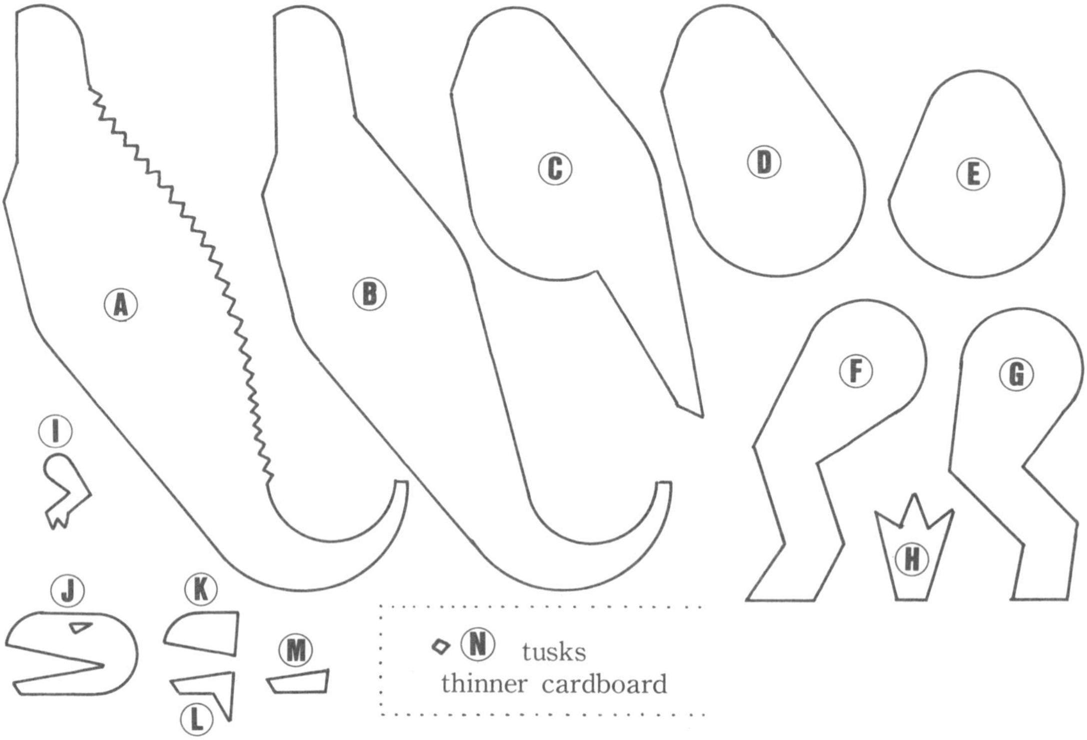

Ⓐ×1 Ⓑ×2 Ⓒ×2 Ⓓ×2 Ⓔ×2 Ⓕ×3 Ⓖ×3 Ⓗ×2 Ⓘ×2
Ⓙ×2 Ⓚ×3 Ⓛ×1 Ⓜ×2 Ⓝ×4 (thinner cardboard)

1

To make the head, first glue the 3 Ⓚ parts together. Next glue the Ⓜ lower jaw parts to either side of Ⓛ. Then, as in the iagram, glue the Ⓙ parts onto all this.
Fold the fangs Ⓝ and glue 2 up and 2 down in the mouth.

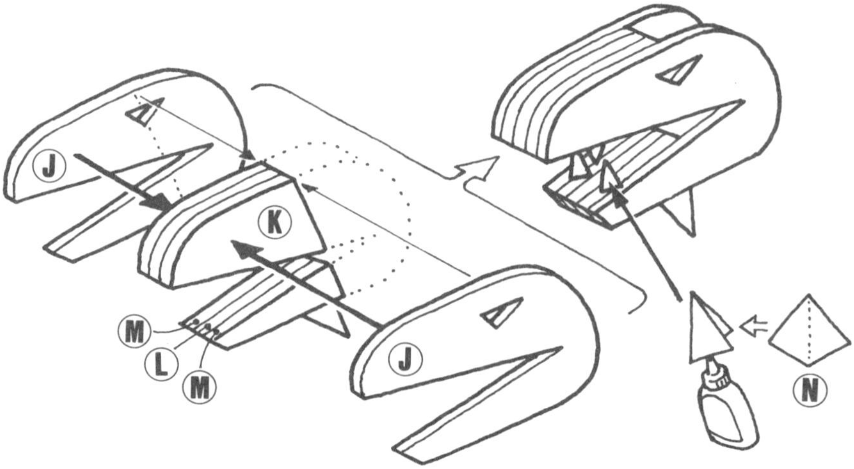

2

To build the torso, put Ⓐ in the middle, and glue onto both sides, in order, the Ⓑ, Ⓒ, Ⓓ and Ⓔ parts. Dab the glue on at $\frac{1}{4}$" to $\frac{1}{2}$" (5mm to 10mm) intervals. Use a triangle to keep everything straight and vertical.

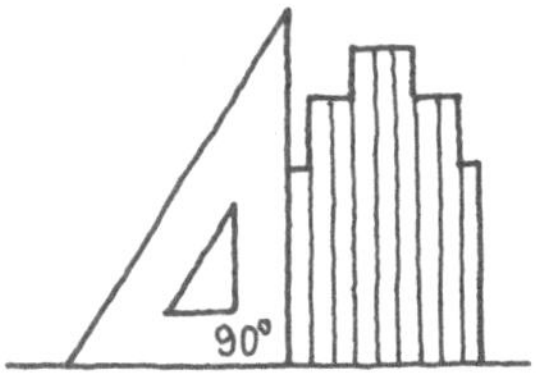

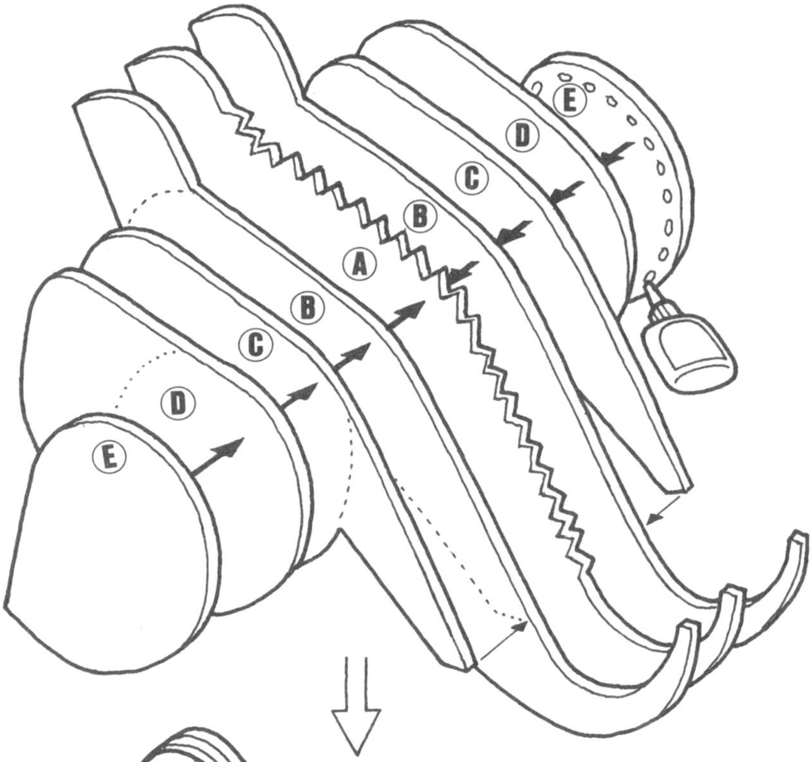

3

Glue the front legs Ⓘ to the torso. Apply glue to the back of the head and attach it to the neck.

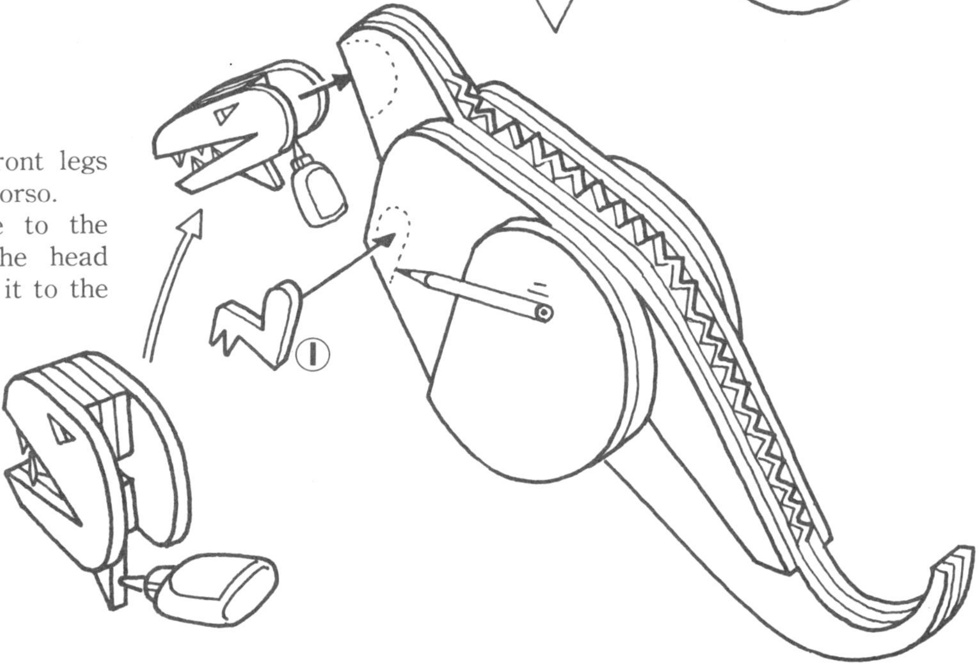

4

Glue the 3 parts of the legs Ⓕ and Ⓖ together, and glue them on to the feet Ⓗ.

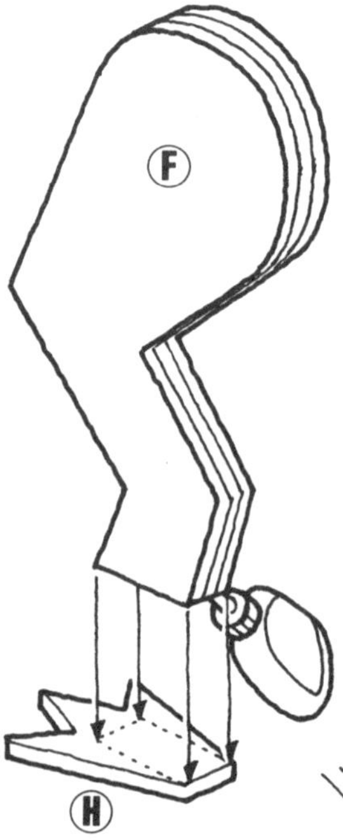

5

Trace onto the Ⓔ parts the location of the legs Ⓕ and Ⓖ, and glue on.

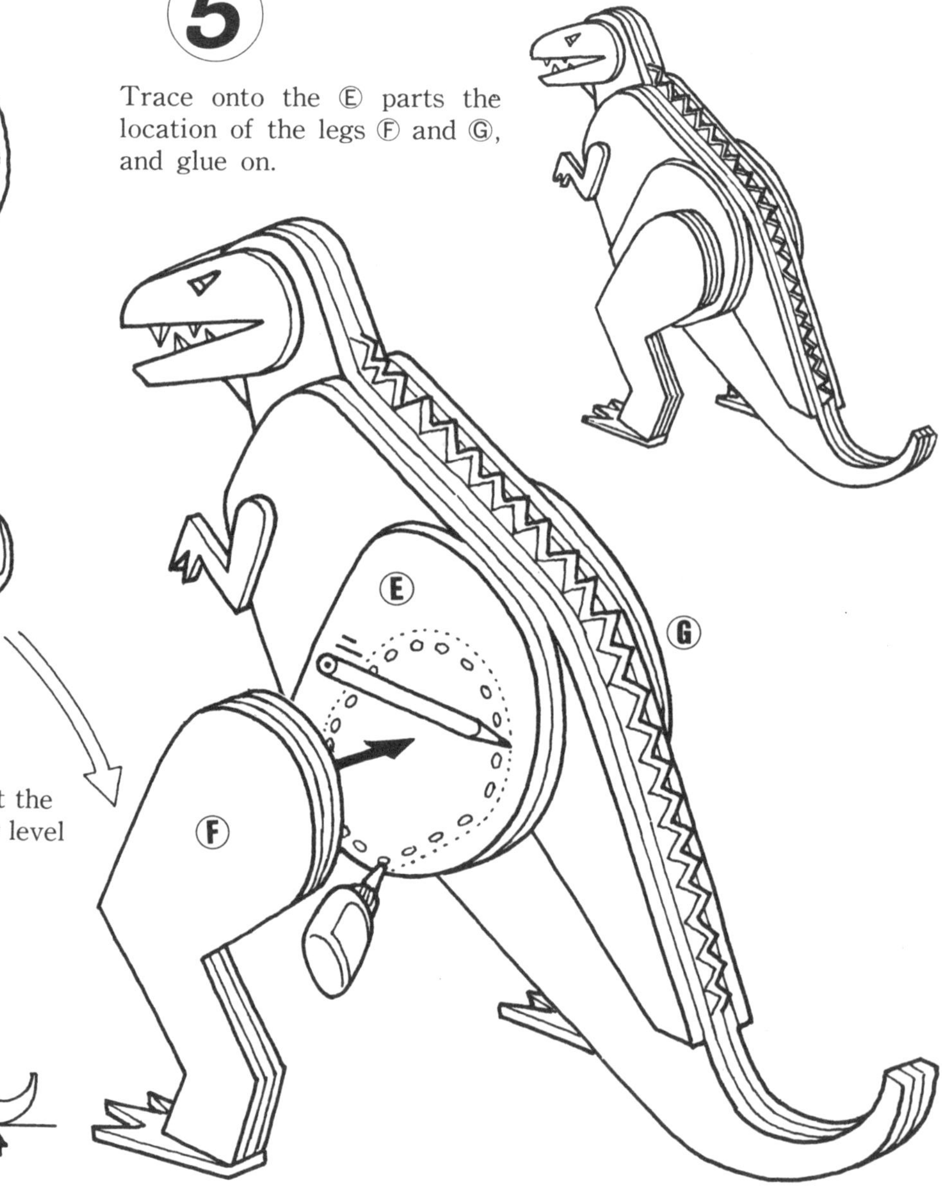

FINISHED

N.B: Make sure that the feet are horizontally level with the tail.

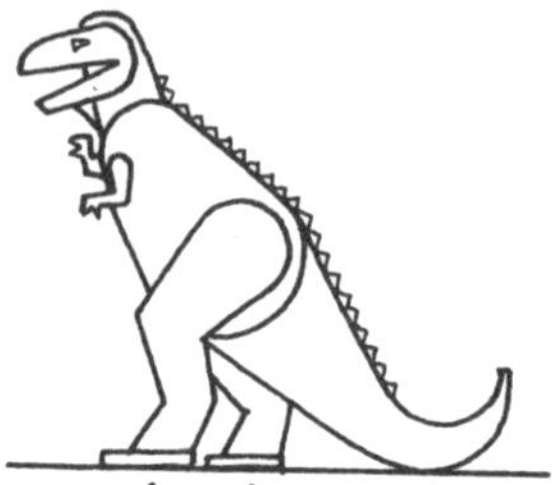

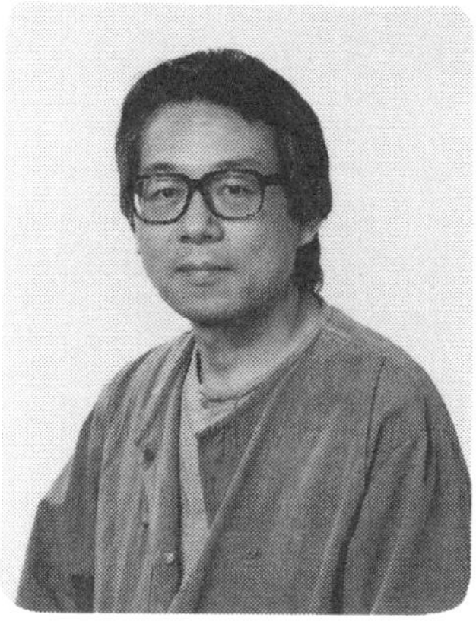

About the author: Hideharu Naito

1944	Born in Yokohama Prefecture, Japan
1967	Graduated in Design from Tama Art University
1968	Awarded Takeo Prize for letterhead design
1972	Established "Naitoh & Wings"
1982	Group exhibition at Shibuya Tokyu Hands
1990	Exhibition of his works at Seibu department store, Ikebukuro
1991	Exhibition of his works at Seibu department store, Tokorozawa.
	Presently known for his work using papercraft and cardboardcraft in advertising, manufactured products, planning and so on.